Israel Horovitz's New Shorts

12 New One Act Plays

A SAMUEL FRENCH ACTING EDITION

NEW YORK HOLLYWOOD LONDON TORONTO

SAMUELFRENCH.COM

Copyright © 2009 by Israel Horovitz

ALL RIGHTS RESERVED

Cover Photograph by Gaëla Blandy
'About the Author' Photograph by Peter Lindbergh
Photographs Appear Courtesy of the Author

CAUTION: Professionals and amateurs are hereby warned that *ISRAEL HOROVITZ'S NEW SHORTS* is subject to a royalty. It is fully protected under the copyright laws of the United States of America, the British Commonwealth, including Canada, and all other countries of the Copyright Union. All rights, including professional, amateur, motion picture, recitation, lecturing, public reading, radio broadcasting, television and the rights of translation into foreign languages are strictly reserved. In its present form the play is dedicated to the reading public only.

The amateur live stage performance rights to *ISRAEL HOROVITZ'S NEW SHORTS* are controlled exclusively by Samuel French, Inc., and royalty arrangements and licenses must be secured well in advance of presentation. PLEASE NOTE that amateur royalty fees are set upon application in accordance with your producing circumstances. When applying for a royalty quotation and license please give us the number of performances intended, dates of production, your seating capacity and admission fee. Royalties are payable one week before the opening performance of the play to Samuel French, Inc., at 45 W. 25th Street, New York, NY 10010.

Royalty of the required amount must be paid whether the play is presented for charity or gain and whether or not admission is charged.

Stock royalty quoted upon application to Samuel French, Inc.

For all other rights than those stipulated above, apply to: Attn: Bruce Miller, Washington Square Arts, 310 Bowery, 2nd Floor, New York, NY 10012; bmiller@washingtonsquarearts.com.

Particular emphasis is laid on the question of amateur or professional readings, permission and terms for which must be secured in writing from Samuel French, Inc.

Copying from this book in whole or in part is strictly forbidden by law, and the right of performance is not transferable.

Whenever the play is produced the following notice must appear on all programs, printing and advertising for the play: "Produced by special arrangement with Samuel French, Inc."

Due authorship credit must be given on all programs, printing and advertising for the play.

ISBN 978-0-573-69609-1   Printed in U.S.A.   #29008

No one shall commit or authorize any act or omission by which the copyright of, or the right to copyright, this play may be impaired.

No one shall make any changes in this play for the purpose of production.

Publication of this play does not imply availability for performance. Both amateurs and professionals considering a production are strongly advised in their own interests to apply to Samuel French, Inc., for written permission before starting rehearsals, advertising, or booking a theatre.

No part of this book may be reproduced, stored in a retrieval system, or transmitted in any form, by any means, now known or yet to be invented, including mechanical, electronic, photocopying, recording, videotaping, or otherwise, without the prior written permission of the publisher.

IMPORTANT BILLING AND CREDIT REQUIREMENTS

All producers of *ISRAEL HOROVITZ'S NEW SHORTS* must give credit to the Author of the Play in all programs distributed in connection with performances of the Play, and in all instances in which the title of the Play appears for the purposes of advertising, publicizing or otherwise exploiting the Play and/or a production. The name of the Author *must* appear on a separate line on which no other name appears, immediately above the title and *must* appear in size of type not less than fifty percent of the size of the title type.

The nine short plays that comprised the Off Broadway show *NEW SHORTS* were produced and performed by The Barefoot Theatre Company, January, 2007, at Theatre Row, New York City (Francisco Solorzano, Producing Artistic Director; Victoria Malvagno, Managing Director). The casts for each play were as follows:

THE BRIDAL DANCE – directed by Michael LoPorto, with special choreography by Yvonne Marceau.

> Roz – Victoria Malvagno
> Dave – Christopher Whalen
> Deb – Kendra Leigh Landon
> Isaac – Francisco Solorzano
> Amy – Maia Sage Ermansons
> Evelyn – Lynn Cohen
> MC – Josh Iacovelli
> Don – Jeremy Brena
> Shelly – Stephanie Janssen

AFFECTION IN TIME – directed by Michael LoPorto.

> Young Woman – Kendra Leigh Landon

THE FAT GUY GETS THE GIRL – directed by Michael LoPorto.

> Binky – Josh Iavovelli
> Cheryl – Victoria Malvagno
> Angry Male Voice – Christopher Whalen
> Angry Female Voice – Kendra Leigh Landon
> Raspy Male Voice (Marv) – Francisco Solorzano

BEIRUT ROCKS – directed by Michael LoPorto.

> Benjy – Christopher Whalen
> Jake – Francisco Solorzano
> Sandy – Kendra Leigh Landon
> Nasa – Stephanie Janssen

AUDITION PLAY – directed Michael LoPorto, with choreography by Victoria Malvagno.

> Alexis – Victoria Malvagno
> Director – Jeremy Brena

HOTEL PLAY – directed by Israel Horovitz.

> Aaron – Jeremy Brena
> Janice – Stephanie Janssen
> Chad – Francisco Solorzano

CAT LADY – directed by Israel Horovitz.

> The Cat Lady – Lynn Cohen

INCONSOLABLE – directed by Michael LoPorto.

> Mother – Kendra Leigh Landon
> Daughter – Maia Sage Ermansons
> Father – Jeremy Brena

THE RACE PLAY – directed by Israel Horovitz.

> Dee Dee Sharp – Lynn Cohen
> Jeannie Rush – Stephanie Janssen
> Announcer – Josh Iacovelli
> Annie Richardson – Maia Sage Ermansons
> Bobbi Levebre – Kendra Leigh Landon
> Evvie Piscato – Victoria Malvagno
> Ernie Philbrook – Jeremy Brena
> Todd McCain – Christopher Whalen
> Jesus Lopez – Francisco Solorzano

The crew and production team for *NEW SHORTS* was as follows:

> Lighting Design – Ji-Youn Chang
> Asst. Lighting Design – Niluka Samarasekera
> Costume Design – Victoria Malvagno
> Sound Design – Tasha Guevara
> Special Choreography – Yvonne Marceau
> Dialect Coach – Nancy Harkins
> Grapic Design – equus, ink.
> Production Stage Manager – Joanna Leigh Jacobsen
> Publicty – Joe Trentacosta, Springer Associates, PR

The plays in this collection originally premiered as two separate evenings of one acts, *New Shorts*, and *6 Hotels*. If theatres desire to recreate these performances, the following 'order of plays' is suggested by the author:

The order of plays for *New Shorts*:

    The Bridal Dance
    Affection In Time (The Prologue)
    The Fat Guy Gets The Girl
    Beirut Rocks
    The Audition Play
    The Hotel Play
    Cat-Lady
    Inconsolable
    The Race Play

The order of plays for *6 Hotels*:

    Fiddleheads and Lovers
    Speaking of Tushy
    Beirut Rocks

    Intermission

    The Audition Play
    The Hotel Play
    2nd Violin

An alternate order includes:

    Fiddleheads and Lovers
    The Fat Guy Gets The Girl
    Speaking of Tushy

    Intermission

    The Audition Play
    The Hotel Play
    2nd Violin

AUTHOR'S NOTE

To perform the entire *New Shorts* evening, exactly as performed Off Broadway, a company of nine actors is required. It can certainly be performed by fewer actors. I suggest that at least two co-directors share the load. Michael LoPorto and I co-directed the Barefoot production (Mike directed six plays, I directed a mere three.). We could have happily used a third partner.

Scenery should be kept to a bare minimum. A bed (on casters) is necessary, plus some utilitarian stage "cubes" that will variously become tables, chairs, etc. I suggest the addition of a couple of rather elegant bentwood chairs. A hotel serving-table (on wheels) is extremely useful for "*The Hotel Play.*"

Actors handle all of the scene-changes. The young actress should be used to introduce each play by its title, directly to the audience, during each scene change...and then announce "Ten Minute Intermission!" between "*Beirut Rocks*" and "*The Audition Play,*" or video projections of titles can be used. If you would like to perform the plays without intermission, you will have to cut two or three plays.

Costumes should be kept minimal to suggest characters, but should always be appropriate and specific...meaning "motif" costumes for "*Fat Guy...,*" running outfits and printed race-numbers for "*The Race Play,*" etc, etc.

Finally, please, bear in mind that doing nine plays – albeit short plays – is nonetheless doing nine plays. So, adequate rehearsal time should be taken. Compare this effort to constructing nine small picture frames. While each frame is small, all nine frame will require the carving of four corners. In parallel, each of these nine plays requires character investigation, sound, lighting – the same basic preparation as a full-length play.

After watching these plays several times, it occurred to me that "*Affection In Time*" could be cut down and serve the evening as its prologue, using the W.H. Auden couplet that ends the play as the evening's theme: "If affection cannot equal be/Let the more loving one be me." (NOTE: I realize that this will place the prologue in second position in the evening, not first. So be it. "*The Bridal Dance*" should definitely be used to open *New Shorts.* Thus, "*Affection in Time*" should be announced to the audience as "*Affection In Time:* The Prologue.")

A new evening, *6 Hotels*, has been fashioned from six of the plays in this collection: "*Fiddleheads and Lovers,*" "*Speaking of Tushy,*" "*Beirut Rocks,*" "*The Audition Play,*" "*The Hotel Play,*" and "*Second Violin.*" All of these plays are, of course, set in hotels.

I directed *6 Hotels* at the Garson Theatre Center's Festival in Sante Fe and then again at Gloucester Stage Company.

I hope you enjoy working on these plays. I loved writing them.

Israel Horovitz
NYC
January 2010

CONTENTS

Bridal Dance 11

Fiddleheads and Lovers. 23

Affection in Time 39

The Fat Guy Gets the Girl. 45

Beirut Rocks 59

The Audition Play 81

The Hotel Play 89

Cat Lady 107

Inconsolable 119

Speaking of Tushy 131

2nd Violin 149

The Race Play. 167

BRIDAL DANCE

THE BRIDAL DANCE was first presented (January 3-27, 2007) by the Barefoot Theatre Co. at Theatre Row, West 42nd St, NYC, in an evening entitled *Israel Horovitz's New Shorts*, directed by Michael LoPorto and Israel Horovitz, choreographed by Yvonne Marceau, with the following cast:

ROZ	Victoria Malvagno
DAVE	Chris Whelan
DEB	Kendra Leigh Landon
ISSAC	Francisco Solorzano
AMY	Maia Sage Ermansons
EVELYN	Lynn Cohen
EMCEE	Josh Iacovelli
DON	Jeremy Brena
SHELLY	Stephanie Janssen

Subsequently, *The Bridal Dance* premiered in France in March, 2009, presented by the Aleas Theatre, directed by Lea Marie-St.Germain.

THE PEOPLE OF THE PLAY

ROZ - late 20s/early 30s.
DAVE - late 20s/early 30s.
DEB - late 20s/early 30s.
ISAAC - late 20s/early 30s.
AMY - 12.
EVELYN - 60s.
SHELLY - late 20s/early 30s, the bride.
DON - late 20s/early 30s, the groom.
EMCEE/DJ - late 20s/early 30s.

THE TIME OF THE PLAY

Night, the present.

THE PLACE OF THE PLAY

Hotel ballroom, working-class NYC suburb.

"...Don José and Donna Inez
A certain kind of marriage led
Wishing each other not divorced,
But dead."

– From Don Juan, by Alfred Lord Byron

(In darkness, we hear – dance band playing wedding music, a waltz, or, easy-listenin'-slow-dancin' rock'n'roll.)

(Lights up on **FOUR COUPLES**, *dancing, chatting, laughing. We are at a wedding in a working-class NYC suburb.)*

(Men wear tuxedo-pants [tux-jackets are off, thus they wear white tux-shirts, bow-ties.] Women wear fancy dresses. The younger women are shoeless.)

(We see – **EMCEE/DJ** *off to one side, wears tuxedo, as well.)*

(Spotlight on – **DAVE** *and* **ROZ**. *Both are in their late 20s.* **DAVE** *is muscular, chews gum.* **ROZ** *is small, full-breasted, pretty-faced.)*

ROZ. How often do you work out, Dave?

DAVE. What are you, *kidding* me?

ROZ. In what sense would I be kidding you, Dave?

DAVE. Let me give you a true fact, Roz…You don't get ripped like I'm ripped, unless you're workin' out every day and doin' doubles on the weekends.

(All freeze. **ROZ** *turns her face front, music stops, as she speaks directly to audience.)*

ROZ. Dave is a major asshole. He dropped out of City College to be a full-time trainer at New York Sports Club. My choices were skip the wedding, come alone to the wedding, or Dave. I fucked up.

(All unfreeze. Dancing and music resume.)

DAVE. *(to* **ROZ**…*)* You must be workin' out quite a lot yourself, Roz.

ROZ. *(All freeze. To audience…)* This will be an idiot-level breast-reference.

(All unfreeze. To **DAVE**...*)*

Why would you think that, Dave?

DAVE. You got yourself a great set of pecs, Roz.

*(***DAVE** *guffaws.* **ROZ** *smiles an "I told you so" to the audience. And then, to* **DAVE**...*)*

ROZ. It's only a gland, Dave.

DAVE. Yuh, for *you*, Roz, maybe, but, for me, they're my favorite vegetable.

ROZ. You're *my* favorite vegetable, Dave.

(Spotlight shifts to – **ISAAC** *and* **DEB**. *He's dark-haired, skinny, intelligent. She's blonde, bone-skinny, pert.)*

DEB. Do you think I look heavy, Isaac?

ISAAC. Excuse me?

DEB. Do you think I look heavy?

ISAAC. You mean, like, *spiritually* heavy kind of thing?

DEB. How can you look heavy spiritually?

ISAAC. I...I don't know. Maybe, like, a-little-too-serious heavy.

DEB. You think I might look seriously heavy?

ISAAC. Wait a minute, wait up! Are you talking, like, you know, *weight*-heavy? Like fat-ass heavy?

DEB. Oh, God! Do you think so, Isaac? Tell me the truth.

ISAAC. Deb, that's a little crazy.

DEB. I don't want to talk about it.

ISAAC. You're a skinny person, Deb.

DEB. Please, don't, Isaac. This is getting me upset. How do you like teaching at Dartmouth?

ISAAC. Fine. Teaching at Dartmouth is fine. I'm actually not a full teacher, I'm a teaching *assistant*. I...

(without pause...)

Deb, do you think you're, like, *fat*?

DEB. Could you not go on with this, please?

ISAAC. I...sure.

(All freeze. ISAAC *turns his face to audience, speaks directly. music stops, as he speaks.)*

ISAAC. Deb eats sponges. She started in high school, and, obviously, never stopped. My across-the-street neighbor, Randy Maloney, went steady with Deb, senior year, had to break it off, because she was grossing him out on a daily basis. She makes herself vomit. They do TV movies of the week about people like Deb. She eats cake and spits it into her napkin...sometimes into her hand. She just did that with a slice of Shelly and Dave's wedding cake, ten minutes ago. We were eating cake and laughing and she just spit her cake into her hand and kept talking to me like nothing happened. Beyond disgusting. She's cute, but she's insane....

(All unfreeze. Music resumes.)

ISAAC. *(to* DEB, *brightly...)* I saw your mother in Starbucks, yesterday morning, Deb. She looks really good. I haven't seen her since senior year. She's really really pretty, your mom.

DEB. Her arms are fat. It freaks me out. If I don't watch it, that's where my arms are going.

ISAAC. Okay. How's your dad doing?

DEB. I don't want to talk about my father, Isaac.

(Beat. And then...)

Have you ever been in treatment, Isaac?

ISAAC. Like, medically?

DEB. Psychologically.

ISAAC. You mean, like, psychotherapy?

DEB. Have you, ever, or are you, now?

ISAAC. No.

DEB. I am. Three times a week.

ISAAC. Really? That's great, Deb!

(to audience...)

My father is a psychotherapist. I happen to be quite close to my dad and I know exactly how he'd react to Deb's long-term body-issues. My dad would say something like "Somebody should track her psychiatrist down and put a knife in his heart."

(to **DEB**...*)*

Is psychotherapy helping, Deb?

DEB. Can I tell you something, Isaac?

ISAAC. Sure, you can.

DEB. I mean something really really personal, something really really really personal...something totally...*out there.*

ISAAC. Sure, Deb. You can tell me anything. Anything.

DEB. We've known each other since 1st grade, right?

ISAAC. I actually moved here in 4th grade, but, whatever.

DEB. I feel I can trust you. Isaac.

ISAAC. You can. You can trust me.

DEB. I'm sleeping with him.

ISAAC. Him who, Deb?

DEB. My doctor.

ISAAC. Your doctor? He's a licensed psychotherapist?

DEB. The sex is amazing.

ISAAC. I can imagine.

DEB. You look quite a lot like him, Isaac.

ISAAC. Like your psychotherapist?

DEB. Like your dad.

*(***ISAAC** *reacts. Beat. And then...)*

(Spotlight shifts to – **AMY**, *a 13 year-old girl, dancing with her grandmother,* **EVELYN**, *60-ish.)*

AMY. How old were you when you met Grandpa?

EVELYN. We were both 12. Almost your age.

AMY. Was it like an arranged marriage kind of thing?

EVELYN. Certainly not! I'm getting old, Amy-darling, but I'm still under 135!

(beat)

We were in junior high school.

AMY. You were in junior high when you got married!?

EVELYN. When we *met*. We were 22 when we got married. Right after college.

AMY. I knew that.

(and then...)

We just studied arranged marriages in my Gender and Sexuality class.

EVELYN. Our marriage was the polar-opposite of arranged. Our parents were dead set against our getting married.

AMY. Why?

EVELYN. Grandpa's parents wanted him to marry somebody from a better family. And my parents wanted me to marry somebody with money.

AMY. Was Grandpa poor?

EVELYN. Then, he was.

AMY. So, why'd they let you get married?

EVELYN. I was pregnant with your father.

AMY. Really! Wow! Does Daddy know that?

EVELYN. I'm not sure he does. Probably not.

AMY. I won't say anything.

(Beat. And then...)

I studied that in Gender and Sexuality, too.

EVELYN. You studied *what* in Gender and Sexuality, dear? The antecedents to your pronouns are not always precisely clear.

AMY. Unwanted pregnancies.

EVELYN. Your dad wasn't at all unwanted. He was extremely wanted. We knew if I got pregnant, they'd have to let us get married. And they did.

AMY. That's so cool!

(and then...)

You should tell Daddy this. I'll bet it will make him really happy to know this...to know for sure he was wanted like that.

EVELYN. I will. It's a good idea, Amy. I *definitely* will.

AMY. If I'm ever in love with someone, I'm going to do the same thing you did, Grandma.

EVELYN. Well…perhaps. Wait and see.

AMY. You must miss Grandpa so much.

EVELYN. I do.

AMY. I do, too.

EVELYN. Thank you for dancing with me, darling. I can't imagine who I'd ever dance with, if I didn't dance with you.

AMY. Somebody's going to ask you to dance with them, Grandma. I'll bet. You're still beautiful, Grandma. And you're a really good dancer.

EVELYN. I hope you're right, Amy, darling, but, I have my doubt.

AMY. No doubt about it, Grandma. Someone's definitely gonna ask you to dance. You wait and see.

(EMCEE enters carrying a mirror-ball and flashlight, spins ball, creating spinning stars, speaks with insincerely joyful, male voice, over microphone.)

EMCEE. Ladies and gentlemen, your bride and groom.

(Applause and cheers from all. Spotlight shifts to – **SHELLY** *and* **DON**, *the bride and groom. She wears bridal gown. He wears Armani tuxedo. They dance as if they'd rehearsed with a professional choreographer, massive spins and dips.)*

(The other couples watch **SHELLY** *and* **DON'S** *elaborate dance-moves, impressed.)*

(After a few moments of spinning and dipping, at the bottom of an amazing dip, **DON** *speaks directly to the audience. All freeze. Music stops as he speaks.)*

DON. *(to audience…)* I have made the biggest fuckin' mistake of my life! She drives me crazy! I've been married for less than two hours and I'm already staring across at Roz's tits, non-stop. I am so not into this! The priest should have said "I now pronounce you man and FIRST wife." We are talking total catastrophe!

(All unfreeze. Music resumes.)

DON. *(to* **SHELLY**...*)* I love you, Shelly.

SHELLY. I love you, Don.

(All freeze. Music stops.)

DON. *(to audience...)* We're doing the wedding rehearsal, yesterday afternoon...I show up in my new Armani tux...twelve hundred bucks, wholesale...she looks at me, goes "Is that what you're *wearing*?!"...Total fucking catastrophe.

(All unfreeze. Music resumes.)

EMCEE. *(over louspeaker)* Time to change partners, ladies and gentlemen! Men move to your left, ladies to your right.

*(***DON*** now dances with* **ROZ**. **SHELLY** *now dances with* **AMY**. **EVELYN** *now dances with* **ISAAC**. **DAVE** *now dances with* **DEB**. *Spotlight on –* **DAVE** *and* **DEB**.*)*

DEB. Do you think I've put on weight, Dave?

DAVE. You are bulking up a little, Deb.

DEB. You think so?

DAVE. Hard to tell when you've got clothes on. You wanna swing by my place, later on, I can have a look at you, give you a professional opinion. I know bodies, Deb. Bodies are kinda my life. Your call?

DEB. I wouldn't mind.

(They slow-dance, upstage. Spotlight on – **ISAAC** *and* **EVELYN**.*)*

EVELYN. How are you enjoying New Hampshire, Isaac?

ISAAC. I like it. I kinda miss my family, though. I kinda hate being so far away, just now.

EVELYN. Why is that?

ISAAC. Since my grandmother died, my grandfather's not doing all that well. I'm really close with him...my grandfather.

EVELYN. I remember that. I knew your grandfather, years back. We were in high school together. Is he ill?

ISAAC. No, he's in great shape. He's just really lonely.

(and then...)

You're a really good dancer, Mrs. Harding.

EVELYN. Thank you, Isaac.

ISAAC. Would you have any interest in going out with my grandfather, if I can pull something together? He loves to dance.

*(Spotlight shifts to – **ROZ** and **DON**.)*

DON. You're looking really wonderful, Roz.

ROZ. I *am?*

DON. Fantastic.

ROZ. Thanks, Don. Coming from a married man, I guess it's sincere.

DON. You're the best-looking woman here by a ton, Roz.

ROZ. A ton?!

DON. I don't mean a ton, in any, like, insanely pejorative way. I mean a ton, like, a ton...like a mile...like, no contest kind of thing.

ROZ. I knew that. Thank you, Don. But, you did just get married, two hours ago. I was here. I saw it happen.

DON. I could be getting it annulled, like, by the end of the day, Tuesday.

ROZ. Is that a joke?

DON. Don't ask, Roz, okay?

ROZ. Okay, I won't. You look really good, too, Don. I love your tux. It's...gorgeous.

*(Spotlight on – **AMY** and **SHELLY**.)*

AMY. You must be soooo happy to be married, Shelly, huh?

*(**SHELLY** begins to sob. Slowly, everyone becomes aware of **SHELLY**'s upset. They stop dancing and watch, as **SHELLY** sobs. She is miserable. She drops to her knees, sobs, moans, sobs and moans.)*

(The lights fade to black.)

The Play is Over.

FIDDLEHEADS AND LOVERS

FIDDLEHEADS AND LOVERS had its world premiere on June 7, 2008, at the Garson Theatre, Santa Fe, New Mexico, in *6 Hotels*, directed by Israel Horovitz with the following cast:

Emma	Marianna Bassham
Noah	Rod Harrison
Elsa	Jane May
Jerry	Joaquin Torres

THE PEOPLE OF THE PLAY

EMMA - 30-40, dark-haired, beautiful.
ELSA - 30-40, blonde, quirky.
NOAH - 35-45, short, quirky.
JERRY - 35-45, tall, handsome.

THE TIME OF THE PLAY

Night. The present.

THE PLACE OF THE PLAY

Restaurant in hotel.

(In darkness, we hear – single cello, sad, and then…)

(Lights up in restaurant, suddenly.)

*(We meet **EMMA**, dark-haired, slim, beautiful, sitting at table opposite **NOAH**, a dentist. **NOAH** is slightly older than **EMMA**, a tad chubby. **EMMA** is mid-sentence…)*

EMMA. …puts my hand on his thigh…*quadracep*…and he kisses me, you know, very, like, *wet*…and he gets this funny kind of confused look on his face, and tells me in this really low, breathy, late-night-FM voice that I taste *plummy*.

NOAH. You are kidding me!

EMMA. I kid you not.

NOAH. Plummy?

EMMA. That's when I knew it was over.

NOAH. Because…?

EMMA. He doesn't kiss me for two years, then, plummy…

(explains)

He forgot he was kissing *me*. He thought…

NOAH. Ohhh.

EMMA. I moved in with my sister for three weeks, then, I found…

NOAH. You have a sister?

EMMA. I do. I'm a twin.

NOAH. That I *really* didn't know. We have twins.

EMMA. I know. I saw the picture.

NOAH. I forgot.

(beat)

It's so weird.

EMMA. What?

NOAH. Just this weird coincidence. Once, when I was first starting out in my practice, I was setting this tricky porcelain veneer on this woman's upper lateral incisor...I'm looking, like, really close, like, nearly *in there*, and she pulls back, goes "Dr. Bellman, your breath smells plummy."

EMMA. That happened?

NOAH. Totally.

EMMA. You're not making this up?

NOAH. Swear to God. Weird, huh? We both get "plummy."

EMMA. She wasn't...? That's not how you met...?

NOAH. Oh, no. I didn't meet her til maybe two years after.

(ELSA enters scene to take order.)

ELSA. Want to stay with flat or bump up to bubbly?

NOAH. Flat's fine.

EMMA. Fine.

ELSA. *(refills water glasses)* Ready to order? I'm not rushing you.

NOAH. Not a problem.

ELSA. Tonight's specials are Fiddleheads Surf & Turf with charcoal grilled hanger steak and skate sautéed in lemon brown butter...$26. Or Dijon Fiddleheads and Mutton...$29. Both specials are served with roasted garlic Yukon mashed potatoes, broccoli rabe and house-grown cardoons.

NOAH. I'll have the Dijon Fiddleheads and Mutton and my friend will have the...

EMMA. I'll go with the same.

ELSA. Good choice. The mutton is outrageous. And the Dijon Fiddleheads are *astonishing*. There is just a touch of non-fat buttermilk in the sauce. I don't know if you're...

NOAH. We're eating mutton.

ELSA. Dumb me. *(slaps her own forehead, laughs)* Of course. Funny. I have to tell Eric.

(and then)

I can recommend an Oriel "Ortolan," Grüner Veltliner, Austrian, 2004, an excellent year for...

NOAH. I prefer a Gigandas.

ELSA. That'll work.

NOAH. *(to* **EMMA***)* You okay with Gigandas?

EMMA. Yuh. Sure. Fine.

ELSA. For a starter, I recommend a salad of poached pears, Gorgonzola cheese and spinach in a black currant vinaigrette, and/or Semolina Dusted Calamari lightly fried with marinara, caper remoulade. They're both yummy.

NOAH. Let's do both. Sounds great.

(to **EMMA***)*

That okay with you?

EMMA. Fine with me.

NOAH. *(to* **ELSA**...*)* The chef knows what he's doing with the Fiddleheads, yes?

(to **EMMA***, explaining...)*

Fiddlehead Fern is, like, poisonous, if you don't cook it exactly right. And they've got to still be coiled, when you eat them. If they straighten out, they can kill you.

ELSA. That's a myth. Undercooked Fiddleheads can be slightly toxic but never poisonous. Eric lives in Hudson, grows his own Ostrich Fern and harvests the Fiddleheads, himself. You can only get sick if they're undercooked. Ten minutes is recommended, we do twelve minutes. So, no worries. My name is Elsa. You are?

(Waits for reply. None is forthcoming, and then...)

EMMA. Oh, uh, Emma.

NOAH. I'm Noah Bellman. Noah. Cosmetic dentistry. Who's Eric?

ELSA. Our owner-chef. This your first time here?

NOAH. Well, sort of.

EMMA. Yes. First time.

ELSA. Well, great to meet you! I'll turn in your orders and if you need anything at all, just, you know, call out my name, I'll come running, you've got a friend…

(smiles)

Carole King.

NOAH. *Love* Carole King. My mother played Tapestry, non-stop, all the time I was growing up.

ELSA. Where'd you grow up?

NOAH. Upper West Side. You?

ELSA. Nevada.

NOAH. Really? I don't think I've ever actually met anybody from Nevada

ELSA. There are a couple of us around. André Agassi. Nevada.

NOAH. He's not Greek?

ELSA. Nevada.

NOAH. Are you, like, *vegan?*

ELSA. Nev-errr! I love great food. "Never eat junk, save it for the good stuff"…That's my motto.

NOAH. Are you an actress?

ELSA. Oh, God, no! I'm a waitress! I had to do some acting to support myself when I first came to New York, until I could find waitress-work. I was glad to have the money. Acting pays well, and it's steady, but, I really hated it. I love waitressing. I know how lucky I am. I'm living the life of my dreams.

(smiles, with special knowledge, madly flirting)

'Course, you know what they say: if we didn't have pigs, we'd never find truffles.

NOAH. *(flirts back as madly)* So true.

EMMA. *(angered by their flirting)* Could you bring us some bread?

ELSA. I could. We bake our own bread. 15 grain with Polenta…Raisin, apricot and fig rolls (dangerous)…

Kale and sweet potato loaf...If you can tell me exactly what and how much you'll want, nothing will be wasted. Save the planet.

NOAH. I'll go for the danger, *comme habitude*. Like, two raisin-apricot rolls, okay?

ELSA. Raisin, apricot and fig. Great choice.

(to **EMMA**...*)*

And...?

EMMA. I'll have that, as well.

ELSA. *(putting Emma down)* Do you always order exactly what he orders? *(icily)* My mother does that.

(And, with that inscrutable remark, **ELSA** *exits.)*

(Beat. And then...)

EMMA. I fuckin' hate her! I hate foodies! Her brain is a shrub.

NOAH. This restaurant is, like, foodie heaven. Foodies and Greenies flock here from all over. I mean, Tamara would have come here five times a week, if I...

EMMA. Three times a week with Jerry.

NOAH. You think?

EMMA. I know she was. His American Express year-end report...

NOAH. Tamara's too...

EMMA. *She* paid?

NOAH. Averaged twice a week.

EMMA. So, his three and her two...

NOAH. Jesus! No wonder she gained weight.

EMMA. From eating here?

NOAH. No, from eating here with him, then coming home, eating again with me.

*(***ELSA*** re-enters with bread and wine. She sets down bread, opens wine, while chatting.)*

ELSA. Four raisin, apricot and fig rolls. If you want more, just call my name...

NOAH. You'll come running.

ELSA. Exactly. Gigondas, 2005, which was an excellent year for anything from the Southeast of France. Please.

(Offers taste to NOAH. He sniffs and sips.)

NOAH. Lovely.

ELSA. Another excellent choice.

(pours out their wine)

Enjoy.

(ELSA exits into the kitchen. NOAH swirls his wine glass, drinks.)

NOAH. Yes. Yes. Gigandas turns me on.

(drinks again)

NOAH. Now, *this* is plummy.

(EMMA sips wine.)

EMMA. I'm tasting apples.

NOAH. Uh uh. I politely but firmly disagree. Anything within 30-35 miles of the Luberon…plummy, not apples.

EMMA. Yuh, well, it's not so important. Can we just say "stand-off"?

NOAH. We could.

(Beat. And then.)

NOAH. So, are you, like, *seeing* anybody?

EMMA. Uh, well, actually, my lawyer doesn't want me to discuss…

NOAH. Oh, *no!* I mean, like, a shrink. Not…

EMMA. Oh! Well…

(She laughs.)

NOAH. What?

EMMA. Can I trust you?

NOAH. Well, sure.

EMMA. I mean really trust you, 'cause this is, well, this is funny.

NOAH. Sure. Absolutely. Funny would be good, because, I don't have a lot of funny going in my life, just now.

EMMA. I, uh, I'm dating my shrink.

NOAH. Is that legal?

EMMA. Why wouldn't it be legal?

NOAH. I don't mean 'legal.' I mean 'ethical.'

EMMA. Ahh. Well. He asked, politely. He's single. His wife died.

NOAH. That's great...That he's single, not that his wife died.

EMMA. I figured.

NOAH. Is it, like, a serious relationship?

EMMA. Oh, God, no! He's well into his eighties.

NOAH. Oh, wow, that's, like, a significant age-difference.

EMMA. Nearly sixty years.

NOAH. That's amazing. And he can still *date?*

(without pause)

I can't believe I just asked you that.

EMMA. It's fine. Don't worry.

(and then...)

It's not...I'm not ready for that, anyway. I mean, he's not uninterested. He's still, you know, vigorous. But, I...

NOAH. I'm not, either. I totally understand. Part of me wants to just, like, go fuck my brains out. Oh, God, sorry! I need an exorcist. My brain and my mouth aren't connected, anymore.

EMMA. Not at all.

NOAH. But, I would only do that to let her know. I mean... you know...to get even.

EMMA. That's a useful insight.

NOAH. It hurts so much.

EMMA. Yes.

NOAH. You trust...

EMMA. I never did. I mean, I always knew he was…I travel, internationally, for my job, so, yuh, I…Honestly, I never minded that part of it. We always had a different set of needs. You see what I'm saying?

NOAH. Absolutely yes. It was exactly the same for us. I never…Not like her. I mean, I'm a dentist, she's a dancer. So, yuh, I sort of *knew*, and it didn't really bother…But, the falling in love part of it.

EMMA. That's the thing.

NOAH. That's the killer.

EMMA. Certainly shocked *me*. When I found the picture of them together with your kids, I knew he…

(Doesn't finish thought. Beat. And then…)

I was screaming at him and I only vaguely heard him say "I'm in love with her"…when it sunk in, my legs went all rubbery. I fell down. He had to help me up. He…

(She turns away, sadly. **NOAH** *watches her awhile, then he reaches across the table, touches her hand, gently. she speaks…)*

EMMA. The only kiss I've had in maybe three years is the plummy…

(beat)

Married nine years, this Valentine's Day. No kids. I agreed to that. Jerry never wanted…He *said* he never wanted…

(beat)

I figure they ate here, then went upstairs, used a room in the hotel. But, they must have used cash for the room, because, there was never…

(She stops talking. A small silence. And then…)

NOAH. Being a dentist's wife couldn't have been, like, so wonderful. I can't forgive her, but, I mean, I'm not so interesting, am I?

(**EMMA** *looks at* **NOAH**, *but, doesn't know what to say.*)

EMMA. Well…I'm sure you have other qualities.

NOAH. I'm seeing a shrink and it's helping. You should… Oh. Right. You said.

(**EMMA** *looks at* **NOAH**, *smiles.*)

EMMA. I'm fine. Really.

(**ELSA** *enters carrying tray with their starters. Serves and chats.*)

ELSA. Calamari…Poached pears…and to celebrate your first time here, Eric has given you a gift of Appalachian ramps, just in season, sautéed in a medley of Ten-of-the-Woods and Chanterelle mushrooms. I had to hold myself back from keeping this for myself. It is *superfly*.

(*smiles*)

Enjoy.

(*Suddenly,* **ELSA** *spots* **JERRY** *entering the restaurant, calls out to him.*)

ELSA. Omigod!…Jerry!…

(**EMMA** *turns, looks. Lights widen to include* **JERRY**.)

EMMA. Oh, my God! Him.

NOAH. Him, who…? *Him!?* You have got to be *kidding*!

EMMA. What the hell was I thinking, coming here?

NOAH. It's a free country.

EMMA. What the fuck does that mean?

NOAH. I don't know.

(**EMMA** *covers her face with her hands, as* **ELSA** *goes to* **JERRY**.)

(*They kiss, and then, Elsa asks discreetly*)

ELSA. Hi, Jerry. Where's Tammy?

JERRY. I'm early.

ELSA. Will you be free, later?

JERRY. I don't know yet.

ELSA. Text me when you know. Ice cold Stella?

JERRY. No, thanks, I'm fine. Tell Eric Tammy and I weren't feeling so great last night, stomach thing. Tammy thinks possibly the fiddleheads were undercooked. She...

(**JERRY** spots **EMMA**. *He is stunned.*)

JERRY. Oy.

ELSA. What?

(**JERRY** *ducks, hides behind* **ELSA**)

JERRY. I, uh, I know her...The woman. There.

ELSA. Who?

(turns, looks)

Emma?

JERRY. I...Her. Yes. My wife.

ELSA. Your *what?* She's...? I thought...?

(realizes)

Oh.

JERRY. I know. I'm sorry I didn't say something. I ws going to.

NOAH. He saw us.

EMMA. Shit!

NOAH. Do you want me to do something?

EMMA. Do what?

NOAH. I don't know.

ELSA. Cripes, Jerry!...Cripes! *(and then...)* I'll go tell Eric you're here.

JERRY. Good. Yes. Good. Tell Eric.

(**ELSA** *exits.* **JERRY** *steps downstage, types out a text message on his iPhone, and waves to* **EMMA**, *smiling, as if pleased to see her.*)

NOAH. He's waving to you. He's, like, calling somebody.

EMMA. *(turns, looks)* He's sending your wife a text message is what he's doing.

NOAH. You mean, like, telling her not to come here, like?

EMMA. Could please stop saying "like"! The 80s are over!

NOAH. Right. Sorry. He's coming over.

(**JERRY** *joins them.*)

JERRY. Hey.

EMMA. Hello, Jerry.

JERRY. I…I'm amazed. You look…

EMMA. Plummy?

JERRY. What?

EMMA. This is Tamara's husband, Noah.

JERRY. Oy.

EMMA. Look at this man, Jerry. You're fucking his wife, and you're fucking up his two kids. You're…

NOAH. No, stop! Shush! Let me. Please. I need to talk to Jerry about Tamara…

(*to* **JERRY**…*looks like a fight is about to happen. And then…*)

Keep the bitch, Jerry. I am so totally over her. I got the kids. You got Tamara. I got lucky.

(**EMMA** *looks up, amazed.*)

NOAH. Most of all, Sport…you dropped a beautiful ball. And I'm pickin' it up!

(*And with that,* **NOAH** *kisses* **EMMA**.)

JERRY. What are you doing?

(**EMMA** *breaks from the kiss, shocked. She looks at* **JERRY**, *then, looks at* **NOAH**. *She kisses* **NOAH**, *passionately, this time.* **JERRY** *watches, flabbergasted. Beat. He turns away, exits the restaurant.* **NOAH** *breaks the kiss.*)

NOAH. Sorry about that. I didn't want to punch him… I need my hands for my work…

EMMA. Again.

NOAH. Really?

(*They kiss, again.*)

EMMA. When's the last time you had sex?

NOAH. A year ago this past Christmas morning. And it wasn't so great.

EMMA. Do you have to be anywhere, after dinner?

NOAH. No.

*(They kiss, again. **NOAH** breaks from the kiss, speaks...)*

You were right. I'm definitely tasting apples.

*(They kiss, again. **ELSA** enters.)*

ELSA. How're we doin' over here?

(sees, realizes)

Oh. Ohhhhh.

*(**EMMA** and **NOAH** continue to kiss.)*

(The lights fade to black.)

The Play is Over.

AFFECTION IN TIME

AFFECTION IN TIME was first presented (January 3-27, 2007) by the Barefoot Theatre Co. at Theatre Row, West 42nd St, NYC, directed by Michael LoPorto, with the following cast:

Young Woman ....Kendra Leigh Landon

THE PEOPLE OF THE PLAY

YOUNG WOMAN

THE TIME OF THE PLAY

The present.

THE PLACE OF THE PLAY

On stage.

NOTE: This play can be used as a possible prologue to evening of New Shorts.

(In darkness, a single cello plays something sampled from Bach's cello concerti.)

(YOUNG WOMAN speaks directly to audience.)

YOUNG WOMAN. If you want to look back in time, you only need glance up at the sky. The sun and the stars are so far from Earth that even at the speed light travels, it still takes a single beam of light nearly 9 minutes to travel from the sun to Earth. So, when we look at the sun, we are actually seeing it as it was nearly 9 minutes ago. And when we look at our next closest star, Alpha Centauri, we are actually seeing it as it was 4.3 years ago. And when we look at extra-galactic stars, we are in fact seeing them from billions of years past. Many of these shimmering stars died out millions of years ago, but we won't live long enough to know it! If the sun disappeared, no one on Earth would know for precisely 8 minutes and 20 seconds!

(beat)

We are, at this moment, in New York City, in a small theatre on West 42nd Street*. The month is January, the year is 2010*.

(beat)

In fact, I am not in New York City*, the month is not January. The year is not 2010*. I am not who you are seeing. I am not a young woman. I am a gray-haired man. I am not in a crowded room with lights shining on me, with eyes staring at me. I am alone.

(beat)

Because of who I am, and what I do with my life, I am able to look forward into history and see this new ending, and the beginning that will follow.

(**NOTE:** Update for each production.)*

(beat)

I cannot possibly alter how you will live your lives on your particular planet. I can only observe. I know that you will call your planet Earth. I know that you will sing and dance, as we did. I know that you will wage war, as we did. I know that you will cause your own destruction, as we did. I know that you will love and hate, as we did. And so, I speak to you now, through time, in your language, to tell you what I have learned from your history and from mine, from your poetry and from mine. And I shall leave you with this thought...one I wish to share with you and with my beloved children...

(beat)

"When affection cannot equal be, let the more loving one be me."

(The music ends.)

The Play is Over.

THE FAT GUY GETS THE GIRL

THE FAT GUY GETS THE GIRL had its world premiere at Gloucester Stage Company, Gloucester, Massachusetts, in July, 2005, directed by Israel Horovitz with the following actors (who later performed the play at the Boston Theatre Marathon, 2006):

Binky . . . . Rick Doucette
Cheryl . . . . Emme Shaw

Subsequently, *THE FAT GUY GETS THE GIRL* was presented in January 2007, by the Barefoot Theatre Co. at Theatre Row, West 42nd St, NYC, directed by Michael LoPorto, with the following cast:

Binky . . . . Josh Iacovelli
Cheryl . . . . Victoria Malvagno

THE PEOPLE OF THE PLAY

BINKY - a.k.a Brian, late 30s, fat.
CHERYL - late 30s, not fat.

THE TIME OF THE PLAY

Night, the present.

THE PLACE OF THE PLAY

Hotel room.

(Extremely tight spotlight on **BINKY**, *a baby-faced fat guy. Really, really fat would be good. He sits up in a hotel bed, covered by a blanket, minutes after sex.)*

(Stage lights will fade up after a few moments to reveal setting. For now, we are tight on **BINKY**'s *face.)*

BINKY. *(middle of a thought, yelling into bathroom.)* You see what I'm sayin'? You walk into a room, *any* room, and if you're, like, last guy in, or maybe even *middle* guy in, there's always this *hate-thing* comin' from the other people who're standin' there. Soon as they look up and see you come in the room, they're goin' 'What's *he* doin' at the party?' Say you're black, there's this Black thing. Say you're a Jew, there's this Jew thing. Say you're a girl with massive tits, there's this *girl with massive tits* thing. Say you're me. *(beat)* You see what I'm sayin', Cheryl?

(By now, the stage lights are in full and we see that we're in a hotel room, and that **BINKY** *is seriously fat. He is naked, but for the bed-sheet around his bottom half.)*

(The room is basic cheap hotel variety, nothing to distinguish it beyond a lack of distinctiveness.)

(We see that the bathroom door is closed, probably locked, Proustian crease of light from inside bathroom is visible at bottom of door.)

(NOTE: *This stage direction shouldn't allow a break in the action.* **BINKY** *simply becomes aware that he has been alone for a long while. He turns to door, calls out, loudly, without hesitation.)*

BINKY. You okay in there, Cheryl?

(No reply.)

BINKY. Cheryl?

(No reply. He calls out, again, more loudly.)

BINKY. Hey, Cheryl!

*(We hear **CHERYL**, from behind closed door.)*

CHERYL. Leave me be.

BINKY. You okay?

CHERYL. Leave me be.

BINKY. You comin' out?

CHERYL. No.

BINKY. How come?

CHERYL. Leave me be.

BINKY. You upset?

CHERYL. Leave me be!

BINKY. You cryin' about something?

CHERYL. Leave me be, Binky, will ya'!

BINKY. You are!

CHERYL. *(sobbing)* Leave me be!

BINKY. Sure.

(beat)

BINKY. You want me to go?

CHERYL. Yes.

BINKY. That's hurtful.

CHERYL. Why'd you ask, then?

BINKY. 'Cause I wanted you to say 'no'.

CHERYL. You asked. I answered.

BINKY. I wanted you to say 'no'.

CHERYL. I said 'yes'. I want you to go. I am not coming out, if you're still there.

(beat)

BINKY. I can't go.

CHERYL. You can.

BINKY. My clothes are in there.

(Beat. Suddenly, the bathroom door opens a crack. We see – **CHERYL***'s hand throwing* **BINKY***'s pants on to the bed. And then, the door closes and locks, as suddenly as it opened.* **NOTE:** *The pants are striped hotel uniform pants, gaudy color.)*

CHERYL. Okay?

BINKY. That is really hurtful, Cheryl.

CHERYL. You got your pants. I'm askin' you to go. I'm not coming out if you're still there, Binky. Now, I'm askin' you, nicely, to get the fuck out of here.

BINKY. Can you tell me why?

CHERYL. Are you going?

BINKY. You've still got my shoes and socks, and my shirt and my cap!

(The door opens. Remainder of **BINKY***'s absurdly fancy uniform is thrown on to the bed – shirt, cap, shoes, socks.)*

CHERYL. Okay? You going, now?

*(***BINKY** *starts to dress himself.)*

BINKY. Can you just tell me what's upsetting you, Cheryl?

CHERYL. Are you leaving, or what? Answer me!

BINKY. *(makes a decision)* No!

CHERYL. "No," you won't answer, or, "No," you're not leaving?

BINKY. No, I'm not leaving.

CHERYL. You've gotta leave, Binky.

BINKY. Why?

CHERYL. Because you've gotta!

BINKY. Just give me a clue.

CHERYL. Please, Binky?

BINKY. Talk to me, Cheryl. Tell me, what's upsetting you?

(beat)

I have feelings for you. I don't want you to be upset.

CHERYL. You know why!

BINKY. I don't.
CHERYL. You do!
BINKY. I don't! I swear I don't!
CHERYL. You do!
BINKY. I *don't*!
CHERYL. You do!
BINKY. I *don't*!

(and then...)

CHERYL. I never did it before, Binky, and you know it!
BINKY. *(chuckles)* That's funny!
CHERYL. What? What's funny? What?
BINKY. *(mock surprise)* You never *did it before*?!
CHERYL. *(annoyed)* You know that!
BINKY. You are *kidding* me!
CHERYL. You know that! You know I never did it before.
BINKY. You did it really good for a first-timer.
CHERYL. *What*?

(and then...)

I hate you!

BINKY. Come on, Cheryl! That was a joke! I'm tryin' to make you feel better!
CHERYL. A joke is funny. A joke makes people laugh. What you just mouthed was nothing like a joke!
BINKY. You sayin' you never cheated on Bob? This is the first time? That's what you're tellin' me?
CHERYL. You know I never did! I would never! Do you think I ever *ever* would?
BINKY. Excuse me, but, you just *did*!
CHERYL. I hate you!
BINKY. Come on, Cheryl, get real! What about Buzzy Peabody? What about Maxie Kendrick? That was not cheating?

*(Sounds of sobbing from **CHERYL**. **BINKY** stands near the door, listening to **CHERYL**'s sobs.)*

BINKY. Hey, Cheryl, c'mon, huh? Talk to me. You hear me? Please, come out and talk to me, Cheryl, huh?

(beat)

Cheryl?

(beat)

Cheryl?

*(Suddenly, the door flies open, knocking **BINKY** backwards. **CHERYL** bursts into the room, enraged.)*

*(**NOTE: CHERYL** wears a uniform that somehow matches **BINKY**'s uniform, thematically. Perhaps their uniforms have a pirate's-motif, or a train-conductor's-motif? Whatever the choice, the uniform should be highly specific and unquestionably absurd.)*

*(**CHERYL** pummels **BINKY** with punches. He falls to the floor and she kicks him with all her might, screaming, furiously. **CHERYL**'s attack should be fierce, and loud.)*

CHERYL. *YOU FAT PIECE OF SHIT HIPPOPOTAMUS! I NEVER SHOULD'VE TRUSTED YOU!*

*(Intercut **CHERYL**'s diatribe with **BINKY**'s defensive screams...)*

BINKY. *CHERYL! STOP! PLEASE! WATCH IT! HEY! STOP IT! CHERYL! STOP IT! WATCH IT! HEY! STOP! CHERYL!*

(Suddenly, there is banging on the wall. We hear – **ANGRY MALE VOICE**.*)*

ANGRY MALE VOICE. *HEY! SHUT IT UP IN THERE!*

BINKY. *(a frightened whisper)* Please, Cheryl, shut up! You're making too much noise!

CHERYL. *(not whispered) I'm* making too much noise? I'm not the only one making noise, Brian!

ANGRY MALE VOICE. *SHUT UP!*

CHERYL. *(yells at* **ANGRY MALE VOICE** *behind wall) YOU SHUT UP, ASSHOLE!*

BINKY. Are you crazy?! You'll get us fired!

(*Thinks about* **CHERYL**'s *boyfriend Bob.*)

You'll get us *killed*!

(**BINKY** *grabs* **CHERYL**, *sits on her.*)

CHERYL. *Get off'a me!*
BINKY. *Be quiet!*

(**BINKY** *yells to the wall.*)

BINKY. Sorry in there! Sorry! We'll be quiet! Sorry!
CHERYL. *Get off'a me, Binky!*
BINKY. *Be quiet!*

(*And now, we hear banging and a* **FEMALE VOICE** *from below.*)

FEMALE. *WILL YOU PLEASE BE QUIET UP THERE?! PEOPLE ARE TRYING TO SLEEP!*

(**BINKY** *yells to the floor.*)

BINKY. *SORRY! SORRY!*
CHERYL. *Get off'a me, Binky!*
BINKY. *Be quiet!*

(*Suddenly, we hear* – *a* **RASPY MALE VOICE** *coming through* **BINKY**'s *walkie-talkie on the night-table.*)

RASPY MALE VOICE. You there, Levine? What the hell are you doin' up there? I thought you were sleeping?!
BINKY. Oh, shit! Somebody called the desk!
RASPY MALE VOICE. (*through walkie-talkie*) Three people called down complaining about the noise, Levine. What are you doin' up there?
BINKY. (*into WALKIE-TALKIE*) I'm sorry, Marv! I'll keep it quiet!
RASPY MALE VOICE. (*through walkie-talkie*) I thought you were takin' a nap!? I thought you were sick?!
BINKY. (*into walkie-talkie*) I was! I am! Uh uh I used the TV for a wake-up and it came on too loud.
RASPY MALE VOICE. (*through walkie-talkie*) Well, shut it off!
BINKY. (*into walkie-talkie*) I did, Marv! I already did!

RASPY MALE VOICE. *(through walkie-talkie)* You're an idiot, Levine!

BINKY. *(into walkie-talkie)* I know, Marv. I'm really sorry.

RASPY MALE VOICE. *(through walkie-talkie)* Hurry your fat ass down here! My shift's up and I've got some action waiting!

BINKY. *(into walkie-talkie)* Two minutes, Marv. I'm just rushing my clothes on.

RASPY MALE VOICE. *(through walkie-talkie)* Over and out.

BINKY. *(into walkie-talkie)* Over and out.

CHERYL. Get your trailer-truck as off'a me! You're gonna squash me!

BINKY. *(whispered)* I'm not movin' til you promise to shut up.

CHERYL. You only get 20 years for rape. You'll get the chair if I die from being squashed.

BINKY. *(whispered)* Shut up, first.

CHERYL. *(whispered)* Fine. Okay. I'm quiet. Now, get up!

BINKY. You promise?

CHERYL. *(quietly)* I hate you!

BINKY. Do you promise?

CHERYL. Yes. I promise.

(BINKY gets off of her. They lie atop bed, side by side, panting, exhausted.)

CHERYL. I really hate you, Brian.

BINKY. Yuh, well, I don't hate you.

CHERYL. Yuh, well, why should you hate me?

BINKY. 'Cause you say terrible things to me.

CHERYL. Oh, *really?* You ever wonder *why?*

BINKY. *(standing, cautiously)* Bobby doesn't love you, Cheryl. He cheats on you all the time. You know he does. You told me he does! You told me yourself about Carole Cardello and him, after you saw them doin' it in his camper-van.

CHERYL. I didn't see them definitely. I only saw that she was in it with him and the van was shaking funny.

BINKY. Get *real*, Cheryl!

> *(slips out, unguarded)*

Bobby doesn't love you, Cheryl. *I* love you.

> *(beat)*

CHERYL. What this?

> *(Beat. **BINKY** is astonished that he's said what he's said. He can't take it back, so he goes with it.)*

BINKY. I've loved you since 3rd grade, in Miss Norton's class. I love you even more, now.

CHERYL. What are you sayin', Binky?

BINKY. The truth, Cheryl. I've never loved anybody else, only you.

CHERYL. What about Mary-Ann Ryan?

BINKY. Besides Mary-Ann Ryan.

CHERYL. I've liked you for a long time, Binky. I wouldn't've come here, if I didn't like you.

BINKY. I know that.

CHERYL. *(looks at her watch)* Our supper's over. We gotta' get back to work. I'm breakin' in a new counter-girl.

BINKY. Will you marry me, Cheryl?

CHERYL. *What?*

BINKY. Will you marry me?

CHERYL. You lost your mind, or what?

BINKY. You're 37, next week, Cheryl. You ought'a be married. And you know it's better to be married to somebody who loves you than to somebody who doesn't. You see what I'm sayin'?

CHERYL. Are you serious on this?

BINKY. On my mother's grave.

CHERYL. Let me think about it.

BINKY. Sure. You don't have to give me a quick answer. There's no hurry on this.

> *(beat)*

It's Sunday night. How about tellin' me Tuesday morning?

CHERYL. *(giggles)* You're crazy.

BINKY. I could take off some weight.

CHERYL. Let me think about it.

BINKY. Should I get the room again for tomorrow?

CHERYL. I dunno.

BINKY. So, why not?

CHERYL. Let me think about it. Ask me, again, before I close up.

BINKY. You're still beautiful, Cheryl.

CHERYL. You're still… *(tries to think of a more flattering word—can't)* nice, Brian. You're a nice guy.

(They kiss. And then…)

CHERYL. This isn't the way I dreamed it, when I was little, Binky. I didn't think my life was gonna' end up like this.

BINKY. Me, neither, Cheryl.

CHERYL. We better get back to work.

BINKY. Maybe I won't give the key in, yet. Maybe we can come back, later, after our shift's up.

CHERYL. Maybe.

(and then…)

Sure.

(Binky smiles, ear to ear. They kiss.)

(The lights fade to black.)

The Play is Over.

(12) NEW SHORTS

BEIRUT ROCKS

The 1st draft of *BEIRUT ROCKS* was given two public readings at The Cherry Lane Theatre, NYC, July, 2006, in an evening entitled *THE MIDDLE EAST: IN PIECES*.

A revised draft was performed at Theatre Row, NYC, January, 2007, in an evening of short plays entitled *ISRAEL HOROVITZ'S NEW SHORTS* presented by The Barefoot Theatre Company, directed by Michael LoPorto and Israel Horovitz, with the following cast:

Benjy . . . . Christopher Whelan
Jake . . . . Francisco Solorzano
Sandy . . . . Kendra leigh Landon
Nasa . . . . Stephanie Janssen

A slightly revised draft of *BEIRUT ROCKS* was performed in the EST Marathon, NYC, June, 2007, directed by Jo Bonney, with the following cast:

Benjy . . . . Enver Gjokaj
Jake . . . . Francisco Solorzano
Sandy . . . . Marin Ireland
Nasa . . . . Stephanie Janssen

A truncated version was performed at the Boston Theatre Marathon in May, 2008.

The current draft of *BEIRUT ROCKS* has been incorporated into a evening of short plays called *6 HOTELS,* which premiered at the Garson Theatre Center, Santa Fe, in June, 2008, directed by Israel Horovitz, with the following cast:

Benjy . . . . Joachiun Torres
Jake . . . . Rod Harrison
Sandy . . . . Jane May
Nasa . . . . Marianna Bassham

Subsequently, *Beirut Rocks* premiered in French language by the Aleas Theatre, Paris, in April, 2009, directed by Lea Marie-St. Germain, and in Greek language by the National Theatre, Rhodes, directed by George Economou.

THE PEOPLE OF THE PLAY

BENJY - early 20s.
JAKE - early 20s.
SANDY - early 20s.
NASA - early 20s.

THE TIME OF THE PLAY

Summer, 2006.

THE PLACE OF THE PLAY

Hotel room, Beirut.

For Jake, who lived it, and Ollie, who told me about it.

(Hotel room, Beirut, Summer, 2006.)

(In the darkness, we hear – the sounds of planes flying overhead, dangerously close. And then...the scream of a missile flying, close by, and then, exploding in distance.)

(Now, we hear the sound of sports commentator's voice. He is covering British Open 2006.)

*(Lights up on **BENJY GERSON**, 20ish year old student, handsome, strong, watching live-action golf on his Mac-Book Pro [portable] computer screen, intently. He holds a golf club in hand, seems excited. He drink from a bottle of Stella Artois. There are two empty bottles on the desk.)*

*(Door opens, **JAKE FEENY** enters, carrying huge backpack, looks worried. Jake's also 20ish, small, baby-faced, cherubic, scared. He wears Red Sox cap, backwards.)*

JAKE. Hi. Okay to...?

BENJY. *(distracted)* Sure. Hi. You speak...?

JAKE. Yuh, yes. Totally. They just sent me up from check-in. I think I'm assigned to this room. Six-sixteen?

BENJY. You got it.

JAKE. I'm Jake Feeny.

BENJY. *(shakes **JAKE**'s hand, absentmindedly)* Benjy Gerson. Hang on...I'm watching live feed...

(screams, suddenly, without warning...)

Holy shit!

JAKE. *(startled by **BENJY**'s scream)* What? What happened? What?

BENJY. Chris DiMarco just dropped a 60-foot putt, saved par. DiMarco could win this! In-fuckin-credible!

JAKE. *(totally confused)* I...uh...

BENJY. British Open. Live feed on PGA.com. Tiger's running away with it, 18 under, all's'a'sudden DiMarco's makes this incredible attack, cuts Tiger's lead to 4. What we're seein here is possibly the greatest Open ever.

(Beat. Smiles.)

Sorry... *What's* your name?

JAKE. Jake. Feeny. I'm from Boston. You?

BENJY. Benjy Gerson.

JAKE. No, I mean, where are you from?

BENJY. Da Bronx.

JAKE. I think I've seen you. You at summer school here?

BENJY. Yuh, American University. I'm doing a 6-week language thing.

JAKE. Me, too. I'm at A.U.B., too.

BENJY. Where are you housed? Were you close?

JAKE. Way close. They put me with a family near the harbor. We were watching out the window...Israeli warships firing missiles...planes flying over real low...The whole house was shaking whenever a bomb hit.

BENJY. *(Watching computer screen; distracted. Suddenly...)* Yes!

(to **JAKE***)*

See, this is Tiger's greatness. DiMarco hits, BAM! Tiger strikes back. BAM! DiMarco's 60-footer's neutralized.

(smiles at **JAKE***, vaguely embarrassed)*

Sorry. I'm really into this. I'm co-captain of my golf team.

(and then...)

I go to Middlebury. You?

JAKE. Harvard.

BENJY. *(probably lying)* I got into Harvard, but Middlebury's package was way better. Plus, the Harvard golf team sucks.

(and then...)

I wanted to play golf for Stanford, bigtime, but, I didn't get recruited, so, ya know, fuck 'em. Bunch'a anti-semites.

(and then...)

BENJY. You must be gettin' a huge rasher of shit in Beirut with a name like Jake? I can cop to "Benjamin," instead of "Benjy," and they're, like, "Hmmmm. Benjamin Franklin, not a Jew"...But, "Jake," no smokescreen. Jake's a definite Jew.

JAKE. I'm not Jewish. I'm half Greek, half Irish.

BENJY. Got that wrong.

JAKE. No probs.

BENJY. You grow up in my part of the Bronx, you figure everybody's either Jewish or Black. Or both. What's your last name?

JAKE. Feeny.

BENJY. Did you already tell me that?

JAKE. I did, yes.

BENJY. I wasn't paying attention. I do that. There's a whole Irish section in the Bronx, just over from us. Irish bars with Irish step-dancing. In this century. It's unbelievable.

(suddenly)

You don't, like, do step-dancing, do you?

JAKE. I do.

(and then...)

I don't.

BENJY. I've got, like, zero people-skills. Birth defect, basically. I was born without a tact gland. What are you studying?

JAKE. Here or at Harvard?

BENJY. Both.

JAKE. Here, Arabic. There, I'm a government major and a language minor. Greek and Arabic.

BENJY. You apply to Stanford?

JAKE. I did.

BENJY. And you got in, right?

JAKE. I did.

BENJY. Yuh, well, good for you. I've gotta' remember I'm doin' okay. I come from nothing. My father's a dry-cleaner in the Bronx. I...*Birdie*! Tiger birdied 15! It's mad emotional, man. Tiger's dad died, couple of weeks ago. DiMarco's mom just died, last week. So, they're both playing on this upper-tier emotional level.

JAKE. You're not so nervous about what's going on here, are you?

BENJY. What do you mean?

JAKE. You think they'll get us out of here?

BENJY. Tonight? Or ever?

JAKE. Tonight, or ever?

BENJY. Don't know about tonight. How many kids came on your bus?

JAKE. To here? Three of us...in a taxi. There were four other taxis, maybe fifteen kids, in all.

BENJY. They won't evacuate us til they have the whole group together. The International SOS guy at the Holding Centre told me this.

JAKE. And you think we're safe here? In this hotel? You don't think this is a logical target?

BENJY. You kidding? You think International SOS is gonna' let 200 American summer school kids get killed? They're insuring the whole program. What's the death settlement? Say two mill per kid. You think International SOS is gonna take a four hundred million dollar hit? I don't think so. Trust me, Jake. We're okay.

JAKE. The Israelis know this?

BENJY. The Israelis know this, Nasrallah knows this, we're okay. Trust me.

(Knock on the door. **JAKE** *and* **BENJY** *exchange a worried glance.* **JAKE** *goes to door, opens it. Two young women wait outside door.* **SANDY** *wears cargo-pants and t-shirt, and* **NASA**, *Palestinian, wears head-dress [face uncovered], long, dark traditional Palestinian clothing. Both carry backpacks, both are really pretty, 20 years old. They greet the boys, politely.)*

JAKE & BENJY. Hi. Hi.

SANDY & NASA. Hi. Hi.

SANDY. Can you tell us where the International SOS room is?

JAKE. Sure. I just came from there. 5th floor, just under us.

SANDY. Oh. Thanks.

JAKE. No probs.

> (**SANDY** and **NASA** exit, closing door behind them.)

BENJY. Arab chick.

JAKE. I think I know her.

> (We hear – sound of planes flying overhead, dangerously close. And then, scream of a missile flying, close by, and then, exploding, nearby hotel.)
>
> (**BENJY** and **JAKE** both hit the deck, covering their heads, as lights dim and restore.)

JAKE. Shit! That was close!

BENJY. We're okay, Jake. Trust me.

JAKE. I don't see me having a lot of choice here, Benjy. Trusting you or not trusting you isn't really in the equation, right now.

> (and then...)

The Lebanese family I've been staying with is supposed to evacuate their house, but, they don't know where to go. Grandfather's 95, in a wheelchair, bunch'a little great-grandkids. The whole neighborhood's been shut down, but nobody's leaving. It's a catastrophe waiting to happen.

BENJY. I'm not sayin' this shit's in any way a good thing, but, two of your soldiers get kidnapped, you gotta' do something or it's not gonna stop. Two goes to four, four goes to eight, do the math.

JAKE. You kidding me?

BENJY. No.

JAKE. Two soldiers got kidnapped 'cause they shouldn't have been where they were, 'cause they're the enemy, 'cause war was declared, like, two thousand years ago.

The Jews are supposed to be an eye-for-an-eye people, right? Well, they're not grabbing two Hezbelloḥ militants, are they? They're killing little kids, families, they're dropping bombs out of the sky! It's murder.

BENJY. Yuh, so…? Hezbollah's firing missiles into Haifa! What's that about?

JAKE. I'll tell you what that's about: that's about three days after Israel bombed Beirut.

BENJY. So, what are you sayin'?

JAKE. I'm saying the Jews are wrong.

BENJY. You sayin' the Jews are wrong or you saying Israel's wrong?

JAKE. I said Israel's wrong.

BENJY. You said "The Jews are wrong"!

JAKE. I *meant* "Israel's wrong"!

BENJY. Wars have been fought for less, my man.

JAKE. You know what I meant.

BENJY. I'm a lit major, Jake. Words are sacred to me. Words are my God.

(We hear – sound of planes flying overhead, dangerously close. And then, scream of a missile flying, closeby, and then, exploding, loudly, closeby. **JAKE** *and* **BENJY** *hit the deck, again. Lights dim and restore.)*

JAKE. This is crazy!

BENJY. Stay calm, Jake. We're gonna be fine. This is not about us.

(looks at screen. Suddenly he screams.)

Jesus! Tiger won it! Inspirational!

*(***JAKE*** is shaken by ***BENJY***'s scream.)*

BENJY. *(watching computer screen quietly)* He's crying. Tiger's got his head buried into Stevie's shoulder…he's sobbing.

(chokes back a sob)

It's emotional. Gets to me. Makes me tear up.

(laughs)

My Mom died when I was in high school.

(beat)

JAKE. My mom just died at Christmas.

BENJY. Whoa. Really? I'm sorry, man.

JAKE. She was nice.

(JAKE sits on bed, upset.)

BENJY. It's the worst. Shit! I'm really sorry. I am.

(beat)

I stick with Israel, probably 'cause I'm Jewish, my folks are big Jews, and, like, deep-down, I'm thinking, "The Holocaust, the Six million, you gotta' be a tough Jew, beats bein' a dead Jew." But, yuh, I can see what you're saying. You hate Bush, yes?

JAKE. 'Course, I do.

BENJY. So, like, I don't really figure all the Lebanese are Hesbollah. Or all Arabs. I know this. I've been staying with a very cool family, this summer. Lebanese Jews, which, of course, turns out to be a total fuckin' oxymoron.

JAKE. Hey, man, I'm Jake Feeny…Irish Greek, who looks a whole lot more Jewish than you do, man.

BENJY. Look at Tiger. Tiger's totally mixed. Part Thai, part African-American with bad Jewish hair…'Course, what's the only thing they see when he shows up at Augusta National?

JAKE. Black man.

BENJY. Black man. World's fucked up.

JAKE. World's fucked up. It costs $45,000 a year to be a government major at Harvard, I work my ass off, get myself a 3-point-8 GPA, and alls I really know for sure is that the world's fucked up.

BENJY. $45,000 a year to be a lit major at Middlebury and "fucked up" is the most poetic expression I can find to describe the world I live in.

JAKE. That's fucked up.

BENJY. Totally fucked up.

(Another explosion, off in distance. **BENJY** *looks out window.)*

BENJY. Why isn't Bush stopping this? Is he that stupid? I mean, the Arabs hate us, already! This makes us look like we're backing it.

JAKE. We *are* backing it! You don't think Israel's making a move without checking with Bush, first, do you?

BENJY. They're making heroes out of Bin Laden and Nasrallah. I saw blogger-kids sayin' this on Protein Wisdom, talkin' about selling tee-shirts with Che Guevera in a tuban wearing bad eye-glasses.

JAKE. You like Dave Chappelle?

BENJY. *(imitates Chappelle)* "I'm rich, bitch!"

(and then, laughing...)

Love Dave Chappelle. Genius.

JAKE. Totally.

*(***JAKE*** and ***BENJY*** slap hands, falsely jovial. Beat. And then...)*

JAKE. We gonna die here, Benjy?

BENJY. Trust me, Jake. International SOS is on the case.

(Practicing chip-shot swing with golf-club, seemingly unconcerned.)

I'm seein' London by midnight tonight. I'm seein' English girls...

JAKE. Can you get news updates on your computer?

BENJY. Yuh, sure...I've been watching CNN online.

JAKE. And?

BENJY. Not a lot of happiness. Tripoli is bye-bye.

JAKE. That's where the family I'm stayin' with's from. That's where they were hoping to go.

BENJY. Not much there to go to.

(We hear – sound of planes flying overhead, dangerously close. And then, scream of a missile flying,

close by, and then, exploding, loudly, nearby hotel. Lights will dim, and then, restore. We hear – ambulances in the distance.)

(**JAKE** *and* **BENJY** *fall to the floor, cover their heads. Protecting themselves. Both are shaken.)*

BENJY. Close.

JAKE. Really close. Jesus!

(Knock on door. The door cracks open, **SANDY** *pokes her head inside.* **NASA** *stands behind her, silently.)*

(Both are frightened.)

SANDY. Hi, again. This is six-sixteen, right?

JAKE. Hi. Yuh. Six-sixteen.

SANDY. I'm Sandy, this is Nasa. We're assigned here 'til the other busses come. Okay for us to come in?

BENJY. Sure.

(**SANDY** *and* **NASA** *enter, quickly.* **NASA** *closes door. They all shake hands, politely.)*

BENJY. I'm Benjamin.

JAKE. Jake.

(to **NASA***)*

You're in my Arabic class, right?

NASA. I am.

JAKE. That's cool.

(to **BENJY***)*

She's in my class. She's smart.

NASA. Thank you.

SANDY. We just met at the holding center. They sent a bunch of us over here in taxis.

BENJY. How many of you in all?

SANDY. Came over? Maybe thirty.

NASA. *(precisely)* Twenty-eight.

SANDY. Twenty-eight. International SOS is supposed to be sending busses for us, later today or tonight, as soon as the whole group's together.

JAKE. To take us where?

SANDY. The International SOS guy's saying probably to Syria. The airport's still open in Damascus.

BENJY. That's what I'm hearing, too. I can get CNN.com online.

SANDY. Are you guys both at A.U.B.?

BENJY. Yuh, you?

SANDY. Uh uh, not me, Nasa is. I'm working on a dig for the summer…archeological dig…The site's south of the city.

JAKE. Wow! You must've been right in the middle of it.

SANDY. Tell me about it! Sooo close. I've been crying for three days, non-stop. I hate Bush, as much as anybody, but, I have to say, I think he walked into an already-fucked-up world. You gotta blame the guy who pulls the trigger, the guy who drops the bomb, the guy who blows himself up on a plane, in a school-bus…I mean, somebody's gotta' be responsible in a real way. All we're finding at the dig is pretty much warriors and weapons. I mean, it's been fucked up here for a long long long time.

*(**NASA** listens, looks, doesn't agree, but says nothing.)*

BENJY. Where do you go to school?

SANDY. I'm an archeology major at Stanford.

*(**BENJY** looks away. **JAKE** smiles.)*

SANDY. How about you guys?

JAKE. Harvard.

SANDY. Oh, I heard the International SOS guy saying that the Harvard kids are getting out first.

BENJY. Middlebury.

SANDY. *(excited by this news)* I've got two cousins at Middlebury.

BENJY. Oh, yuh? What's their names?

SANDY. Alice and Sophie Collins? They're gonna be sophomores in September…Twins, really cute.

BENJY. *(thrilled to make this connection)* I know them! Alice and Sophie Collins! That's amazing!

*(We hear – sound of planes flying overhead, dangerously close. And then, scream of a missile flying, close by, and then, exploding, close by. Everybody falls to the floor to protect themselves – except **NASA**, who stays upright, hands covering her ears. The lights flicker, dim.)*

SANDY. Oh, God! That's close!

JAKE. That's the closest.

NASA. They won't stop! They will never stop!

BENJY. Stay calm. We're in a safe-house.

SANDY. Personally, I don't think a hotel with a couple of hundred privileged American college-kids waiting for evacuation is exactly a safe-house, Jake.

JAKE. I'm Jake, he's Benjy.

SANDY. Sorry.

JAKE. Easy to tell us apart: Benjy's the one who's not shaking.

BENJY. *(moving to bed, carrying golf club)* Believe me, Bush and Cheney have got this one covered. 200 American students get killed in Beruit, their approval-rating plummets. They're not gonna let this happen. Too close to an election year. Trust me.

NASA. *(cannot stay silent)* The missiles are American missiles. The Jews are using American missiles.

BENJY. Excuse me? You mean 'the Jews" or you mean 'the Israelis'?

NASA. What's the difference?

BENJY. Uhhh, there IS a difference. Where are you from?

NASA. I was born in Palestine. I grew up in Massachusetts.

JAKE. I'm from Massachusetts. What town are you from?

NASA. Medford. You?

JAKE. I'm from Wakefield. What brought your family to Medford?

NASA. I was raised by my mother's cousin. She's a professor at Tufts.

JAKE. You go to Tufts?

NASA. No.

JAKE. Where do you go?

NASA. I'm taking time off.

JAKE. Oh.

BENJY. How come you're studying Arabic, if you're, ya' know, personally Arabic?

(All are startled by Benjy's racist remark.)

NASA. I grew up speaking English. I never studied Arabic, before, this year.

JAKE. Wow! First year? That's impressive. You're doing great with it.

(to all)

She's the smartest one in my class by a mile.

(and then...)

Where were you in school before you took time off?

NASA. In England. At Cambridge.

JAKE. Wow! Cambridge. That's amazing.

SANDY. *(to NASA)* That's amazing, Nasa! I didn't know that.

(to all)

We just met, yesterday.

(We hear – sound of planes flying overhead, dangerously close. And then, scream of a missile flying, close by, and then, exploding. This one is really close. Everybody [except NASA] falls to floor, covering their heads.)

(The lights flicker, dim, restore. Immediately, there is another missile, another bomb, even closer. Everybody [except NASA] falls to floor.)

JAKE. Shit!

BENJY. That was close.

SANDY. *(crying)* Oh, my God! Oh, my God! Oh, my God! That was so close! Sorry. I tend toward a little hysteria.

(We hear – sound of planes flying overhead, dangerously close. And then, scream of a missile flying, close by, and then, exploding, even closer, even more loudly.)

(Everybody [except **NASA**] *falls to floor, covering their heads.)*

(The lights flicker, dim, restore.)

NASA. They will never stop. They want everybody dead.

BENJY. Who 'they'? Who wants everybody dead?

NASA. The Jews.

BENJY. Excuse me, my name's Benjy Gerson. I'm a Jew. I don't want everybody dead.

NASA. Dead or enslaved. What's the difference?

BENJY. Excuse me. You didn't answer *my* question. I'm asking if you think the enemy is Israel or Jews in general.

NASA. I heard your question.

BENJY. So, what's your answer?

NASA. Jews, specifically, not generally. When the world is free of Jews, the world will be free.

BENJY. *(Stunned. He laughs.)* Am I hearin' you right?

NASA. Why? You think you wouldn't support the killing of all Arabs?

BENJY. You're fucked up.

NASA. Try to control your language.

BENJY. *(angrily)* Fuck you.

JAKE. Hey!

SANDY. Come on, you guys! We're all in this together.

BENJY. She should be on her knees, begging my forgiveness! She should be on her knees, sucking my dick!

SANDY. Hey!

JAKE. Hey, Benjy, that's enough! Chill out!

(to the girls)

I just met him, ten minutes ago.

BENJY. *(furious with* **JAKE***)* Fuck you, too, man! You're with them! You'd blow my mother up, same as her. She's a Jew-lady.

JAKE. You're talking shit, Benjy. I wouldn't blow your mother up.

(NASA *is at the bed, about to search for something in her backpack.*)

NASA. It would give me great pleasure to blow your mother up. It would give my life purpose.

BENJY. What's your purpose today?

(*He sees* NASA *open her backpack. Is there as bomb inside?*)

BENJY. *WHAT'S YOUR FUCKIN PURPOSE TODAY?!*

SANDY. Oh, my God!

JAKE. Hey!

(NASA *reaches for her backpack. Suddenly,* BENJY *leaps atop bed, shoves* NASA *aside, threatens to hit her with golf club.*)

BENJY. *(screams at* NASA*)* You make one move with your hands, bitch, you die, bitch! *YOU HEAR ME?!*

(*He carefully inspects contents of her backpack.*)

JAKE. Jesus, Benjy, stop! What are you doing?!

(BENJY *hops down from bed, satisfied backpack doesn't contain a bomb. He stares at* NASA*'s loose-fitting robe. And then...*)

BENJY. She's wired! This bitch is wired! She's goin' for 7th fuckin' heaven! Aren't you, bitch?

(NASA, *terrified, runs toward the door.* BENJY *chases her, threatens to hit her with his golf club.* SANDY *backs away from* NASA, *frightened.*)

BENJY. One move, one move, I send your brain out the back of your head, bitch!

(BENJY *is poised to hit* NASA *wih golf club.* NASA *cringes in fear as* BENJY*'s rage is evident.* SANDY *is crying.* JAKE *is in a state of shock, tries bravely to stop* BENJY.*)

JAKE. Benjy, you gotta listen to reason, man. We're all totally stressed out from this. There's gonna be consequence from what you're doing. There's...

BENJY. *(out of control)* She's wired, you asshole! She's gonna kill 200 American University of Beirut fuckwits! She's wired, asshole!

JAKE. She's not wired.

(to NASA)

Tell him.

NASA. *(to BENJY, angrily)* Kill me, Jew. Kill me. Do it!

BENJY. Lift her skirt up, Jake.

JAKE. What?

BENJY. Her "Bubka" or "Burka" or whatever the fuck it is!… Lift it, Jake! Show me she's clean. Show me this Arab bitch isn't wired. Do it!

JAKE. No way, Benjy! You wanna hit me with your golf club, hit me. No way am I doing this!

BENJY. *(threatening to kill NASA with golf club)* Do it. Do it!

(screams)

DO IT!

SANDY. *(screams…)* *I'LL DO IT!*

(to BENJY)

I'll do it.

(to NASA)

Let me do it, Nasa. Just let it happen.

(and then…)

You don't have anything under there, do you?…I mean, like a bomb kind of thing…? I know you don't. I believe you. I do. Just let this happen, okay?

BENJY. *(golf club raised above NASA's head)* Listen to her! Move one finger and your head's a stain on the wall! *You get me?!*

SANDY. Let me do this, please, Nasa. Just let me do this. Just let this happen. Please?

NASA. Do it.

*(**SANDY** kneels in front of **NASA**, slowly lifts **NASA**'s robe. **NASA** wears pink underwear decorated with tiny pink hearts, and a matching bra…sweet, colorful, typically American.)*

(Her stomach is bare. No bomb. **SANDY** *lowers* **NASA***'s skirt.* **NASA** *straightens her skirt, turns toward the wall, sobbing.)*

SANDY. There's nothing. She's got nothing. I believed you, Nasa. I really did. I'm really sorry.

JAKE. Jesus!

SANDY. There's nothing.

(yells at **BENJY***)*

She's got nothing!...

JAKE. Jesus. Jesus Jesus Jesus.

*(***NASA** *sobs, humiliated beyond words.* **SANDY** *is weeping, moves to* **NASA***.)*

SANDY. I'm sorry. I'm really sorry. Please...

*(***NASA** *turns, spits at* **SANDY***, hits* **SANDY***'s face.)*

SANDY. Nooo, please, nooo!...I'm sorry! I'm really sorry! It was possible. It really was possible.

*(***SANDY** *sobs, sits on bed.)*

JAKE. *(moves to* **NASA***)* I'm sorry, Nasa. I'm really really sorry. That was terrible. That was really terrible.

*(***JAKE** *touches* **NASA***'s shoulder.* **NASA** *swats his hand away, betrayed, furious.)*

JAKE. *(to* **BENJY***)* Say you're sorry to her, Benjy. Tell her you made a mistake.

(kicks bed, angrily)

Say something!...

BENJY. *(to* **JAKE***, simply, calmly)* Fuck you.

(Suddenly, **BENJY** *slams golf club against top of bed, four times, violently.)*

BENJY. Fuck you fuck you fuck you fuck you!

(There is a silence. **BENJY** *stares at* **NASA***.* **SANDY** *also watches her, weeping. Beat. And then...)*

NASA. *(A mixture of rage and tears)* My family was killed by an Israeli missile that was fired from a tank into our house. I was two and a half. I had three older brothers. We lived in Gaza. My father owned a laundry. Many of his customers were Jews. One of his workers was a Jew. I'm told that my father hated politics. I'm told he was a peaceful man. He was killed, instantly, so were my brothers, my grandmother and grandfather. I was sleeping in a cot behind the house. They died. I didn't die. The Israelis thought there was a Hamas leader living in the house. They had the wrong address. They killed my family. Hamas paid for their burial. My mother's cousin came to collect me and take me back to America. All through high school, I thought the Palestinians were wrong. I thought Hamas was wrong. I thought I was American and the Israelis were the good guys. Last year, I began to think for myself, and I realized that I am not American. I am Palestinian. I am an Arab. I am studying my people's history, and learning our language. I want to know my family, my mother and father and brothers. I only have photographs and they look very nice.

*(to **BENJY**)*

You should have killed me, because I have a plan. I will be a martyr…I will honor my mother and father, I will honor my brothers, I will honor my grandparents. Sooner or later, it will happen.

(in Arabic, chanted, loudly, head raised to Heaven:)

God is great. Hamas is great. Allah hu akbar. Hamas hu Akbar. Allah hu akbar. Hamas hu Akbar.

*(in English, to **BENJY**)*

You should kill me. If you don't, I will kill your family. Sooner or later, it will happen.

(We hear – sound of planes flying overhead, dangerously close. And then, scream of a missile flying, close by, and then, a bomb, exploding, close by.)

(The back wall and windows glow red, silhouetting **NASA**, *standing upright, proud, ready to die.)*

(The lights fade to black.)

The Play is Over.

THE AUDITION PLAY

THE AUDITION PLAY was first presented (January 3-27, 2007) by the Barefoot Theatre Co. at Theatre Row, West 42nd St, NYC, choreographed by Victoria Malvagno, directed by Michael LoPorto, with the following actors (who later performed the play at the Boston Theatre Marathon, 2007):

Alexis . . . . Victoria Malvagno
Director . . . . Jeremy Brena

The current draft of *THE AUDITION PLAY* has been incorporated into a evening of short plays called 6 HOTELS, which premiered at the Garson Theatre Center, Santa Fe, in June, 2008, directed by Israel Horovitz, with the following cast:

Alexis . . . . Jane May
Director . . . . Joachin Torres

THE PEOPLE OF THE PLAY

ALEXIS - 30s.
DIRECTOR - a/k/a ED, 30s.

THE TIME OF THE PLAY

The present.

THE PLACE OF THE PLAY

Hotel ballroom, NYC.

For Victoria and Frank.

(In darkness we hear, single piano playing something appropriate for accompanying a slow jazz-tap dance-audition.)

(We now hear the tap-shuffle-shuffle-tap of a single dancer's tap-shoes/feet.)

(Tight spolight on – **ALEXIS***, tapping her way through a fairly complicated dance-routine, which she will continue performing throughout entire play.)*

(After a few moments, we hear – **DIRECTOR***'s voice, offstage, over loudspeaker, or sitting in front of the stage in shadows.)*

DIRECTOR. *(Heavy Boston "Pahk-yo'r -cahr" accent)* Where were you born, Alexis?

*(***ALEXIS*** continues to dance...answers with heavy Queens accent.)*

ALEXIS. Where was I born?

DIRECTOR. Yes. Where were you born?

ALEXIS. Boston*.

(*pronounced "Bor-stin")

DIRECTOR. Boston?

ALEXIS. Yuh. I was born in Boston*. Why?

DIRECTOR. You've picked yourself up a kind'a wicked awful New York accent, somewhere along the line.

ALEXIS. Yuh, well...it happens.

DIRECTOR. Does it go away?

ALEXIS. Does what go away?

DIRECTOR. The accent. The show's set in the deep South.

ALEXIS. I know the show's set in the deep South. I do deep South. I've done a lot of deep South.

DIRECTOR. Like...?

ALEXIS. Like a lot of stuff. It's on my resumé.

DIRECTOR. Tell me out loud, and do a heavy deep South when you tell me. Okay?

ALEXIS. Sure thing. No problem.

(Switches to accent that's a blend of deep South and deep Long Island City.)

Uh, well, ah did deep South in a lot of stuff…

DIRECTOR. Like…?

ALEXIS. Ah did deep South in "Ah Streetcar Named Dee-zi-ah"…bah Mistah Tennessee Willyums.

DIRECTOR. I'm not seeing "Streetcar" on your resumé, Alexis. Where'd you do "Streetcar"?

ALEXIS. In Boston.

DIRECTOR. Really? I'm *from* Boston. Who'd you do "Streetcar" for?

ALEXIS. *(lying)* Outside of Boston. A little theatre on the Cape.

DIRECTOR. Which one?

ALEXIS. Which Cape?

DIRETOR. Which theatre.

ALEXIS. Little summer theatre. You probably never heard of it.

DIRECTOR. I worked summers on the Cape for ten years.

ALEXIS. Yuh, well…We were a kind of *restaurant* theatre. In a fish restaurant.

DIRECTOR. Who directed it?

ALEXIS. I can't remember. My cousin Elliot.

DIRECTOR. Elliot Engel?

ALEXIS. Elliot Palumbo.

DIRECTOR. I don't think I know him.

ALEXIS. Yuh, well, he died. Tragically.

DIRECTOR. I can imagine. What happened?

ALEXIS. Car wreck.

DIRECTOR. How old was he?

ALEXIS. Old. He shouldn't have been driving.

DIRECTOR. You have an adaptation of "Gone With the Wind" listed. Where'd you do that, Alexis?

ALEXIS. Same place.

DIRECTOR. Elliot Palumbo direct that one, as well?

ALEXIS. He did, yuh.

DIRECTOR. Looks like just about everything you've listed here is set in the deep South.

ALEXIS. Yuh, well, the show's deep South, so, I gave you my deep South credits. Something wrong with that?

DIRECTOR. *(amusement in his voice)* No, that's fine, Alexis. Were most of these shows in the same fish restaurant?

ALEXIS. Yuh. They were. Yes.

DIRECTOR. Elliot Palumbo productions?

ALEXIS. Yuh. Uh huh. Yuh.

DIRECTOR. Before his tragic accident?

ALEXIS. No, after he was *dead*! Can I ask you why accent is such a big deal here? I'm auditioning for dance-chorus, for non-speaking roles.

DIRECTOR. The dance-chorus is gonna yell things from time to time.

ALEXIS. Like what kind've things?

DIRECTOR. I dunno…things. Deep South things.

ALEXIS. How's my tap-routine?

DIRECTOR. Fine. Your tap-routine's fine.

ALEXIS. I'm auditioning for dance-chorus.

DIRECTOR. It's just the accent-thing, that's all.

ALEXIS. What do *you* know about deep southern shit? You're from Boston. You sound like a Pepperidge Farm bread commercial!

DIRECTOR. Are any of these credits real, Alexis?

ALEXIS. *(does energetic tap routine throughout speech, ending in a huge finish)* What you're seein' is real, isn't it? My routine is real, isn't it? You need proof of what you're seein'? I've been raising kids for thirteen years. You got kids, Ed? *(beat)* You had a mother, right? Well, I've been one of those for thirteen years. Before that, I was doing nothing but taking dance class and acting class and voice class…For fifteen years, I've been doin' mother-shit and nothin' else, on my own, no husband…raising two kids on my own, workin' 45 hours in a restaurant near my house…but I've been dancing and singing in my living room, every night, Ed. That's your name, right, Ed? Ed? I've been rehearsing, non-stop. I haven't missed a night in thirteen years, Ed. I'm ready. My kids do good in school – Aggie's in 5th grade, Julie's in 7th. They're good kids. They know it's time for me to do something for myself and they're okay with it. I talked this through with them and they're okay with it. Your show's happening close enough to the F-train for them to come over, if they have to. I wanna' do this show, Ed. You're not gonna' meet anybody in the world who's gonna' wanna' do this show more than I wanna' do this show. It's a non-equity showcase in a hotel, Ed. You're payin' zero money.

(Big finish, ends in a split.)

Gimme a fuckin' break, will ya, Ed?

(beat)

DIRECTOR. Can you come back in for callbacks, tomorrow, Alexis?

ALEXIS. I can.

DIRECTOR. Let's do that, Alexis. How's 2:30?

ALEXIS. 2:30's fine, Ed.

DIRECTOR. Excellent.

(The music stops.)

*(**ALEXIS** stops dancing. She smiles.)*

(The lights fade out.)

The Play is Over.

THE HOTEL PLAY

THE HOTEL PLAY was first presented at Theatre Row, NYC, January, 2007, in an evening of short plays entitled *ISRAEL HOROVITZ'S NEW SHORTS*, produced by The Barefoot Theatre Company, directed by Israel Horovitz, with the following cast:

Janice	Stephanie Janssen
Aaron	Jeremy Brena
Chad	Francisco Solorzano
Don	Jeremy Brena

The current draft of *THE HOTEL PLAY* has been incorporated into a evening of short plays called *6 HOTELS,* which premiered at the Garson Theatre Center, Santa Fe, in June, 2008, directed by Israel Horovitz, with the following cast:

Janice	Marianna Bassham
Aaron	Rod Harrison
Chad	Joachin Torres

THE PEOPLE OF THE PLAY

AARON - 40s.
JANICE - 30s.
CHAD - 30s.

THE TIME OF THE PLAY

Midnight. The present.

THE PLACE OF THE PLAY

Hotel room, NYC.

For Stephanie Janssen.

(Lights up in hotel room. Sound of shower running in bathroom, off, bathroom door mostly closed.)

(We are seeing – **AARON**, *40s, tall, handsome, dressing as quickly as he can, as quietly as he can. He counts out four $100 bills from his wallet and places them on the bureau-top. He exits thru main door, quickly, quietly, closing door behind him. He is gone. Beat.)*

(The room is now seemingly empty. We are seeing... unmade bed, rumpled bed-clothing, women's clothing on chair – jeans, top, jacket – shoes on floor, nearby.)

(Car-keys and $400 cash sit atop of bureau.)

(Sound of shower stops. Beat.)

*(***JANICE***'s voice calls out.)*

JANICE. Aaron?...You just say something?

(Beat. Door opens. **JANICE** *pokes head into room, hair dripping wet, looks around. She's beautiful.)*

JANICE. Aaron?

(She is obviously upset to realize that she is alone. She disappears into bathroom. Beat. She enters main room, towel on head, wearing hotel-owned terrycloth robe.)

(Knock on door. She looks up, hopefully.)

JANICE. Aaron?

(We hear – **CHAD'S VOICE**, *other side of door.)*

CHAD. Room service.

JANICE. *(obviously disappointed)* Oh. Right.

(Closes robe, sits, calls out.)

Okay! Come in!

(Stands, fastens robe more tightly closed.)

CHAD. *(off)* Okay to come in?

JANICE. Sure. Yes! Come in!

(Door opens. **CHAD** *enters, wheeling serving table, set with food for two people. He is in his late 20s-early 30s, pretty-faced, athletic.)*

CHAD. Hi.

JANICE. Hi.

CHAD. Where do you want this?

JANICE. I don't care.

CHAD. How's by the window?

JANICE. Fine.

CHAD. It's okay by the window?

JANICE. I just said 'fine'.

CHAD. Sorry. I didn't hear you.

JANICE. By the window's great.

CHAD. Great.

(and then...)

I can put it someplace else. No problem.

JANICE. By the window's fine.

CHAD. Fine.

(He wheels table to window, sets up the two meals.)

JANICE. It's okay. I can do that.

CHAD. I've got it, really. You want the candle lit?

JANICE. What? Oh, yuh, sure. Great.

(He lights candle.)

CHAD. Perfumed. Smell it?

JANICE. I guess.

CHAD. Lily of the Valley.

JANICE. Right. Nice.

CHAD. My mother used to wear Lily of the Valley perfume.

(beat)

CHAD. *(cont.)* I didn't pick it. It's a coincidence. Lily of the Valley's the hotel's official smell – *scent.*

JANICE. This hotel has an official scent?

CHAD. An official color...official flower...official spring-water...scent. Don't ask me. I just work here.

(and then...)

Whenever I light a candle, I think of my mother.

JANICE. Is she dead?

CHAD. Uh uh. She just lives in Connecticut.

JANICE. *(smiles)* My parents live in Connecticut.

CHAD. Oh, yuh, they do? I was just making a joke. I've got nothing against Connecticut. Whereabouts?

JANICE. My parents? You know Connecticut?

CHAD. Not so much, no. I didn't grow up there.

(looks around room)

Want me to keep these plates covered?

JANICE. Doesn't matter.

CHAD. Is he coming right back?

JANICE. Who?

CHAD. I...Sorry. I didn't mean...

JANICE. I don't...

CHAD. I just thought...

JANICE. It's okay, really...

CHAD. I saw him and...

JANICE. You did?

CHAD. I did. Yuh.

JANICE. How long ago?

CHAD. Just now. When I was coming out of the elevator with the table...

JANICE. He was getting in?

CHAD. Maybe six minutes ago. He held the door for me. Seemed like a nice enough guy. Smiled, goes "What's up?" He could have just gone out for something. I mean...Sorry...

JANICE. No, really...I don't...Really.

(**CHAD** *finishes the meal set-up.*)

CHAD. So. There it is. I'll open the wine, so it can breathe.

JANICE. Sure. Great.

CHAD. Gigondas...hotel's official red.

JANICE. Great.

CHAD. From the Luberon region of France...near Avignon. Big-bodied, plummy...with a hint of Crimini mushroom.

(smiles)

We have to know these things. We get quizzed.

JANICE. You hungry?

CHAD. Oh, right, no...I can't...

JANICE. Who's gonna' know?

CHAD. I...well...You sure?

JANICE. I'm sure.

CHAD. Has to be quick.

(and then...)

You really sure?

JANICE. Believe me, I...

CHAD. *(sitting)* The Wild Salmon's the best thing they've got. The veggie is grilled fiddlehead fern. Just came into season. And this vintage is...really good. Red's totally inappropriate with salmon, but, really good.

JANICE. *(sitting)* I'm Janice.

CHAD. I'm Chad.

(and then...)

I made it up. I mean, my real name's something else. I found Chad. Chad and Jeremy? 60s rock duo. Brits.

JANICE. I think so.

CHAD. "Yesterday's Gone," "A Summer Song," "Willow Weep For Me," "Four Strong Winds."

JANICE. Oh. Right.

CHAD. You're...?

JANICE. Jeremy. No. I'm Janice.

CHAD. You said that. I'm Chad. I said that. Well...*now*, I'm Chad. I was born Alvin.

JANICE. Really.

CHAD. You see what I'm sayin'?

JANICE. Alvy's okay.

CHAD. You think? Go for it. Call yourself 'Alvy'. I'm gonna' stick with Chad.

JANICE. Janice is kind've Alviny.

CHAD. It is. If I were Janice I'd probably lose it, go with something like, I dunno, Angelina.

JANICE. My last name's Farina.

CHAD. Right. Okay. We don't do Angelina.

JANICE. My last name's not Farina. My last name's something else.

CHAD. Schwartz?

JANICE. How'd you know that?

CHAD. On the food order. Schwartz in Eleven-Seventeen.

JANICE. Right.

CHAD. You sure he's not coming back?

JANICE. Eat.

CHAD. You from out of town like?

JANICE. Not for a long time.

CHAD. Oh, so...

(spots the $400 on bureau)

What's your deal?

JANICE. What's *your* deal? Actor?

CHAD. Yuh. Well...yuh. I had work three weeks, last year, two weeks the year before that.

(and then...)

If I eat, you've gotta eat, too.

JANICE. I'm not hungry.

(and then...)

You have a girlfriend?

CHAD. Not.

JANICE. Boyfriend?

CHAD. Neither.

JANICE. How come?

CHAD. Gets in the way of the work.

JANICE. This?

CHAD. Yuh.

JANICE. Bellhopping?

CHAD. I'm in the same line of work you're in.

JANICE. I'm not following something.

CHAD. I'm basically doing what you're doing. You're just obviously doing it better than me.

JANICE. I'm *seriously* not following.

CHAD. I'm seeing $400 on the night-table.

JANICE. Oh, nooo. That's for the room. Ohhhh. You think I…ohhh, no, I…

(and then…)

That's what you do?

CHAD. I do, yuh.

JANICE. Oh. Well. That's cool.

CHAD. You approve?

JANICE. I don't disapprove. I mean, it's your life, Al…right?

CHAD. I get two-fifty.

JANICE. It's money for the hotel room. I…

(and then…)

Maybe I *am* better at it than you are.

CHAD. Could be.

(and then…)

Am I making, like, a big big mistake, here? I mean, is he like your husband kind of thing?

JANICE. He's, like, somebody else's husband kind've thing.

CHAD. And you like *know him*?

JANICE. Uh, yuhhh…I do know him.

CHAD. Oh. Ohhhh. Slow. You name your kid Alvin, slow is what you get.

JANICE. We've been doing this for four years.

CHAD. This? Oh, right. Meeting in hotels kind of thing.

JANICE. He leaves the room money, I pay the hotel on my credit card and at the end of the month, I pay American Express…

CHAD. …With his four hundred bucks…

JANICE. Whatever the room costs. We usually meet downtown, but, he had this meeting uptown, so we tried… here.

CHAD. That's cool.

JANICE. You approve?

CHAD. I don't *dis*approve.

(and then…)

Four years is a long time.

JANICE. It's not something I enjoy quantifying. So…Chad… You, like, do it with people for money?

CHAD. I do.

JANICE. In hotel rooms.

CHAD. In hotel rooms.

JANICE. Women come here for that?

CHAD. Women and men.

JANICE. Oh. Ohhh. Right.

CHAD. They don't necessarily come here for that…but they're here, usually for some business shit, and they're lonely, and it's a quick hundred fifty…

JANICE. You use condoms, right?

CHAD. Are you friendly with my mother?

JANICE. What? Oh. Right. No, I'm sorry, that just like *came out*. Not my business. I do that…talk, then think. In that order.

CHAD. Are you not eating?

JANICE. Are you friendly with my mother?

CHAD. Possibly. She ever stay here on her own?

JANICE. Hilarious.

> *(eats)*

CHAD. You like it?

JANICE. Great.

> *(and then…)*
>
> I'm not a huge fish person.
>
> *(Beat. And then…)*
>
> *He* is.
>
> *(and then…)*
>
> How long have you been doing this?

CHAD. Working here, or, this line of work?

JANICE. Both.

CHAD. Here, almost three years. This line of work, about six years.

JANICE. Right. It's cool.

> *(and then…)*
>
> That's a long time.

CHAD. Quantify all you want.

JANICE. Do you ever, like, *date*?

CHAD. Date? Like…what?…Like, tonight's Bingo night at Burritoville kind'a thing? No. Not for a while.

JANICE. I can understand that.

CHAD. Good. Always nice to be understood.

JANICE. I just meant…never mind.

CHAD. I had a girlfriend for a while, maybe eight-nine months. Then, I had a boyfriend for a while, about a year.

JANICE. Cool.

CHAD. You don't really think it's cool. You're really wondering "Which one did he like better?"…

JANICE. That's ridiculous!

> *(beat)*
>
> Which one?

CHAD. Marginally, the boy. When he got annoying, I could hit him and not feel guilty. I could never hit a girl.

JANICE. I have to say, Al, that is seriously fucking admirable.

CHAD. I can't stick with anybody. Girl, boy, doesn't matter. It's like some weird form of A.D.D. I had this nice little dog, once, Cairn terrier named Murphy…gave him away after three months.

JANICE. Dogs aren't easy.

CHAD. Try not to say baldly supportive shit, okay? It annoys me.

JANICE. You have a really low annoyance threshold.

CHAD. I do.

JANICE. That annoyed you.

CHAD. It did.

JANICE. Did you have, like, a really tough childhood?

CHAD. I had a really *annoying* childhood.

JANICE. It shows.

(**CHAD** *stands, goes to* **JANICE***, seems to want to kiss her.*)

JANICE. What are you doing?

CHAD. I'd like to kiss you.

JANICE. Probably better not to, okay?

CHAD. I'd like to.

JANICE. I can't afford you, Chad.

CHAD. That wasn't annoying. That was straight up harsh.

JANICE. Yuh, well, moving from four years with a married father of three girls to a male bellhop-hustler could possibly end up being just a little harsh for me.

CHAD. Don't you ever think "There's a reason for this"?

JANICE. For this *what?*

CHAD. For this fact. For this, "He walks out, I walk in, within four minutes we're eating wild Salmon, the hotel's official fish, we're laughing, we're trading state-fucking-secrets…

JANICE. The reason I'm here is because I sleep with a married advertising account supervisor who had one kid when I started working for him, two kids when I started sleeping with him and, now, he's got three kids, and he wants out. In fact, he *is* out, he *walked* out.

CHAD. Before or after?

JANICE. What would be your guess?

CHAD. Can I kiss you?

JANICE. *Why?*

CHAD. Because I think you're really really smart and really really nice.

JANICE. Yuh, well, you're wrong, I'm not.

CHAD. Can I kiss you, Jeremy?

JANICE. No!

>*(and then...)*
>
>You can hold me. We can hug. I can use a hug.
>
>*(They hug. It is a long tender embrace.)*
>
>*(JANICE begins to cry.)*

JANICE. *(as she sobs...)* Fuck! I wasn't going to cry! This is totally your fault!

CHAD. Life is a piece of shit.

JANICE. *(laughing and crying)* "Life is a piece of shit"?

CHAD. *(laughs)* You've never read Beckett?

JANICE. Beckett said, "Life is a piece of shit"?

CHAD. *(mock surprise)* Beckett *didn't* say, "Life is a piece of shit"?

JANICE. Come here.

>*(She kisses CHAD. It is a sweet kiss. They break from the kiss, but continue to embrace.)*
>
>*(JANICE resumes crying.)*

JANICE. I'm sorry.

CHAD. Don't be sorry.

>*(CHAD begins to cry, as well. JANICE feels his tears on her cheek.)*

JANICE. *(through her tears...)* Are you crying, too?

CHAD. *(through his tears...)* Shut up. You're annoying. I'll smack you.

JANICE. *(sobbing)* How did we fuck up our lives? We're both smart. Did you go to college?

CHAD. Wesleyan.

JANICE. There. See? I knew it. I went to Sarah Lawrence. So, how did we make our lives such fucking miseries?

CHAD. *(sobbings)* Is that Beckett?

JANICE. *(laughs)* Joyce.

CHAD. Shit!

JANICE. What?

CHAD. Joyce's my *mother's* name.

(They share a laugh. And then, they kiss.)

(The door opens. **AARON** *enters the room holding his hotel key-card.)*

*(***JANICE** *and* **CHAD** *pull back from each other.)*

CHAD. Not good.

AARON. Perfect.

JANICE. Aaron, this is Chad, Chad, this is Aaron.

AARON. Perfect. I'm out'ta here twenty minutes...

JANICE. Aaron, I...No! I'm not sorry, I'm not sorry, I'm not sorry. You left. Why'd you come back?

AARON. To talk. I fucking came back to fucking talk to you! I was dumb enough to think we could talk.

CHAD. Bullshit! You came back for your car-keys.

(to **JANICE***)*

His car-keys are on the bureau.

*(***CHAD** *goes to bureau, gets* **AARON***'s car-keys, reads key-tag.)*

Paramus Suburu.

(tosses keys to **AARON***)*

CHAD. This time of night, you should get a clear shot over the bridge, pal. Take you no time.

(**AARON** *clenches his fist, makes a move to hit* **CHAD**.)

I wouldn't recommend fucking with me, pal. I'm a lot tougher then you.

(**AARON** *comes at* **CHAD**, *who throws a punch, misses.* **AARON** *hits* **CHAD** *with a left jab, then decks him with a right to the sweet spot.* **CHAD** *goes down in a heap against the wall.*)

CHAD. *(to* **JANICE**, *rubbing his jaw)* That didn't work.

(to **AARON** *)*

Okay, I'm out'ta here.

(**CHAD** *goes to door, exits.*)

JANICE. You forgot your fucking car-keys!?

AARON. That's not the only reason I came back, Janice.

JANICE. Go home, Aaron.

AARON. I don't want to.

JANICE. You have to.

AARON. Four years.

JANICE. Go. Please, Aaron. Go.

AARON. We tried.

JANICE. You go or I'll go.

AARON. If I hadn't come back in, then, would you have fucked him?

JANICE. Yes.

AARON. I don't know what to say.

JANICE. Say, 'goodbye'. Say, 'It was a mistake'. Say, 'I've got three little girls waiting for me at home, this was crazy.' And go, Aaron. Please, Aaron. Don't pull me back into this. I hate this.

AARON. I…I'll go. You have the money for the room.

JANICE. Take the money. I don't want the money.

AARON. It's $600.

JANICE. I can afford $400. It'll make me feel a whole lot less stupid. Take your money, Aaron, please.

AARON. Where is it?

JANICE. It's on the...

(*JANICE now realizes that the $400 is gone.* **CHAD** *took it.*)

JANICE. Oh, God!

AARON. The bellhop *took it*?

JANICE. *(holding back tears)* Aaron, go. Please, go. If you have any feelings for me at all, you'll go. Please, Aaron... That's all I want from you. Go home. Please.

AARON. I...

(He doesn't finish his thought. He moves quickly to door, exits.)

(Long beat. **JANICE** *doesn't move.)*

(**JANICE** *goes to the table, sits, drinks wine.* **SHE** *is weeping.*)

(There is a knock at the door. **JANICE** *looks up, hopefully.)*

CHAD *(off)* Room service.

(**JANICE** *looks up, confused.*)

JANICE. Come in.

(The door opens, **CHAD** *re-enters.)*

CHAD. Get dressed. I've got four hundred bucks we can blow. Tonight's bingo night at Burritoville. You wanna?

(**JANICE** *smiles.*)

(The lights fade to black.)

The Play is Over.

(12) NEW SHORTS

CAT LADY

The earliest draft of *CAT LADY* was presented by Gloucester Stage Company, August, 2005, directed by Israel Horovitz, with the following actor (who later performed a truncated version of the play the The Boston Theatre Marathon 2006):

Cat Lady . . . . Nancy Carroll

Subsequently, the NYC premiere of *CAT LADY* was at Theatre Row, NYC, January, 2007, in an evening of short plays entitled *ISRAEL HOROVITZ'S NEW SHORTS*, produced by The Barefoot Theatre Company, directed by Israel Horovitz, with the following cast:

Cat Lady . . . . Lynn Cohen

THE PEOPLE OF THE PLAY

CAT LADY – an old woman, long white hair, multi-layered, scruffy clothing.

THE TIME OF THE PLAY

The present.

THE PLACE OF THE PLAY

A beach.

In memory of Murphy, a dog, and Mr. Pokey, a Guinea Pig.

(In darkness, we hear…)

CAT LADY. Here, Puss! Here, Puss-puss-puss!

(Music in…Bach, played by a single cello, loud, elegant, terrifying…)

(Single spotlight fades up on…old lady, on beach, calling out to her missing cat. There is a park bench, center, and an overturned aluminum walker, upstage-right.)

NOTE: *Actress can also start play by crawling about beneath the feet of various audience members, looking for her cat.*

CAT LADY. Here, Puss! Here, Puss-puss-puss! Here, Puss! Here, Puss-puss-puss! Here, Puss! Here, Puss-puss-puss!

(The stage lights switch on, suddenly, startling her. She blinks in the light, sees audience, speaks…)

CAT LADY. You cannot trust a cat. They have too many lives. There is no ultimate threat to a cat. You can't threaten to kill them, unless you threaten to kill them nine times, because they've got nine lives, so, they couldn't care less. And if you actually kill them, they just come back. Of course, if you hang around through seven or eight of their lives, they only have a couple left, and they start to get a little nervous, but, not really.

(beat)

Many people think that cats having nine lives is a myth – an old-wives' tale – but, it's true. I've seen it. I *lived* it.

(beat)

My cat – Cabbage – ran away, two days after I found her. I say *found her*, but, I didn't actually find her. She found me. She walked through my bedroom window. Somebody had abandoned her, I suppose. Anyway, she chose me. I was sleeping. It was summer, hot, I was in my bed with the window open. I was dreaming and I had this sense of somebody staring at me. I opened my eye and Cabbage was on my pillow. Her nose was pressed right up against mine. She was tiny, all gray, like an old baby.

(Beat. She calls out to the missing cat...)

Here, puss-puss-puss! Here, puss-puss-puss!

(beat)

I called her Cabbage because she *ate* cabbage. I know cats aren't supposed to eat cabbage. They're supposed to eat fish. But, my cat hated fish. Wouldn't touch the stuff. She loved *cabbage*. Cabbage stuffed with meatballs was her favorite, but she would also munch raw cabbage, and with great enthusiasm.

(beat)

I also love cabbage – cabbage, the vegetable, not Cabbage, the cat. I suppose I love Cabbage, the cat, as well. I don't *feel* a great deal of love for this particular cat, but I suppose I must *have* love for her, because she's been with me for so many years. I can't remember how many, exactly. A lot. I wasn't young when she came to me, but – well – I wasn't young 40 years ago, was I?

(beat)

I suppose I've also had a lot of lives. I was first married when I was 16. I was actually *15*, when I got pregnant, and 16 when I got married. I was still 16 when I got divorced. The baby was still-born, a still-birth. I went the full 9 months, and delivered him in the normal fashion. A little boy...perfectly well-formed, quite beautiful, but, definitely dead. I felt him die, several days before he was born. He was kicking, furiously, and then, nothing. I went to the doctor for confirmation, but, I had no doubt. My stomach had been full of life, large, robust – and then, it was just, you know, soft, lifeless, like a sack of bones.

(Beat. She calls out to the missing cat...)

Here, puss-puss-puss! Here, puss-puss-puss!

(beat)

My parents and my boyfriend's parents all celebrated the erasure of this sin. I said, "my boyfriend." I meant to say, "my husband." It's difficult to talk of a 14 year-old as "my husband." Especially, now, when I'm nearly 100. He was only 14, when I got pregnant.

(beat)

I can't actually remember his name.

(beat)

Not my husband's. My husband's name was Billy. I mean the son, the baby – the *dead* baby. Neal. We named him Neal. It wasn't anything official, of course. You're not allowed to name a dead baby anything. The name Neal was just something between us – something we decided...my husband and me. Officially, Neal was in the record-books as "The dead baby."

(Beat. She exits stage, looking for cat.)

Here, puss-puss-puss! Here, puss-puss-puss!

(She re-enters, talking a blue-streak.)

My second marriage didn't last much longer than my first. I was married to a bus driver. He left me, six months after we were married. Drove away, bus and all, never came back. It was a city bus. We were living in Boston, at the time. I was 19, when I married him, and 20, when he drove away.

(beat)

The police couldn't believe I wasn't involved, implicated in his crime. I don't mean his leaving me was a crime. I mean the taking of the bus.

(beat)

I wonder who was on the bus with him? I'd never thought of that, before. There might have been innocent people on the bus — school children...shoppers. Fancy that!

(Beat. She calls out to the missing cat...)

Here, puss-puss-puss! Here, puss-puss-puss!

(beat)

I didn't marry again until I was 25. I wasn't allowed to. There was a court order, in fact, preventing me from marrying again – a sort of statute of limitation. The police never really believed he'd left me. They thought we were still partners – partners in crime. A team of bus thieves. After 5 years, they gave up looking for the bus and my husband. As did I.

(beat)

I turned 25, and re-married, immediately. My new husband – Alfred – never learned to drive. That was fine with me. Alfred tried to learn. He went to many, many driving schools. He was desperate to learn, but, he failed his driving test, 7 or 8 times. No motor-skills, you might say. Poor Alfred was afflicted with a rare astigmatism. He was both far-sighted and near-sighted. He was far sighted in his right eye and near-sighted in his left eye. On top of that, he was totally colorblind. Everything appeared blue to poor Alfred. Life was so difficult for him. It's difficult not to feel blue when everything else actually *is* blue. Alfred was constantly depressed. So much so, I couldn't stay married to him. I left him in our 13th month. I went into then bedroom to tell him I was going, but I found him crying. So, I said nothing. I just left.

(Beat. She calls out to the missing cat...She exits the stage.)

Here, puss-puss-puss! Here, puss-puss-puss!

(Beat. She re-enters, speaking as if she never stopped speaking.)

It's upsetting, when you leave things you love, or when things you love leave you. Even things you don't love.

It's always upsetting. Coupling and uncoupling. Both so difficult.

(beat)

My 4th and 5th marriages were catastrophic. Both husbands died, within a year of the wedding bells. George was the first. Well, the 4th, actually, but the 1st of the two who died. We never knew if he died of natural causes, or if there was foul play. There was a noose around his neck, which certainly opened the door to suspicion. Richie, my 5th husband, put his head in the oven. It was horrible. Shocking. Electric stove. He was *roasted*!

(Beat. She calls out to the missing cat...)

Here, puss-puss-puss! Here, puss-puss-puss!

(beat)

My 6th husband Roger and I stayed in the throes of marital bliss for more than 40 years, from the time I was 27 til I was 66, nearly 67. We had two sets of twins and a set of triplets.

(beat)

That's 2 and 2 and 3 – 7 kiddoes, in all, plus, of course, Cabbage.

(beat)

Roger's gone, the kiddoes are all gone, as well.

(beat)

It's not such a great thing to live as long as I've lived. You pay a terrible price.

(beat)

Two of the kiddoes went in a car wreck. Roger and the other kiddoes lived long lives and died. One of the triplets – Allen – he only went til 48. Not really a long life. His brothers went 'til 70, and died within two days of each other. Roger — my husband – was nearly 90 when his heart gave out.

(beat)

He left me alone with the cat. Many women are left alone with a cat. Men seem to be left alone with dogs and women with cats. This is a theory I would explore, if I were younger.

(Beat. She calls out to the missing cat...)

Here, puss-puss-puss! Here, puss-puss-puss!

(beat)

We were together, all those years, Cabbage and I. It difficult to know if the accident were my fault, or Cabbage's fault. Not important, I suppose. It seemed important, at the time.

(beat)

We often came to this beach, to take the air. I love the sea. Cats, I suppose, are not sea-lovers like people. Let me be honest: I don't love the sea. I love the sea*side*. Here, Cabbage and I are in total accord. I never liked the sea, never liked the idea of waves lapping my legs. I never liked wet. But, I've always adored the beach, the sand. And how could Cabbage not adore the sand, as well? It's a giant cat-box, after all, totally liberating for a cat, I should imagine. I've relieved myself many time in the sand. Most people relieve themselves in the sea, but, I have always found that to be most unpleasant.

(Beat. She calls out to the missing cat...)

Here, puss-puss-puss! Here, puss-puss-puss!

(beat)

When we crossed the street from the beach to the bus, Cabbage bolted away from me. I tried to stop her, but she was a cat who could not be convinced of anything. Once her mind was set, she never wavered. She wanted to bolt, and she bolted. I saw the car hit her and it was horrible. First the front wheels, then the back wheels. And then, as if that weren't enough, the crazy bastard backed up to see what he'd done – rolled over her, one more time. I was *dumbstruck*, really dumbstruck.

(beat)

And that's how it happened.

(beat)

I moved into the road, toward the poor flattened cat, and saw nothing of the bus but the bus-driver's eyes, wide as saucers. I remember the thud of the bus hitting me. I remember my flight through the air to the sand. I remember thinking "This is quite fun." And then, nothing.

(beat)

Could I have been thrown so far that I've not yet reached the spot where the cat lay dead, or has she moved into her ninth life and run off, again? It's so difficult to know.

(Beat. She calls out to the missing cat...)

Here, puss-puss-puss! Here, puss-puss-puss!

(beat)

I've been walking for days and days, calling and calling, but, there's no sign of her.

(beat)

She'll come back. She always comes back. She would never leave me alone. Never alone.

(Beat. She exits, rolling walker, calling out to the missing cat...)

Here, puss-puss-puss! Here, puss-puss-puss! Here, puss-puss-puss! Here, puss-puss-puss!

(The lights fade out.)

The Play is Over.

(12) NEW SHORTS

INCONSOLABLE

INCONSOLABLE was first presented (January 3-27, 2007) by the Barefoot Theatre Co. in an evening of short plays entitled *ISRAEL HOROVITZ'S NEW SHORTS*, at Theatre Row, West 42nd St, NYC, directed by Michael LoPorto, with the following cast:

Mother . . . . Kendra Leigh Landon
Daughter . . . . Maia Sage Ermansons
Father . . . . Jeremy Brena

THE PEOPLE OF THE PLAY

DAUGHTER - a.k.a EMILY, 13.
MOTHER - a.k.a EMILY, mid 30s/early 40s.
FATHER - mid 30s/early 40s.

THE TIME OF THE PLAY

Scenes alternate between the present and flashbacks to 32 years earlier.

THE PLACE OF THE PLAY

Family home.

In memory of Philippa Adams Davidson.

(In darkness, we hear a single cello, hauntingly sad. Lights up on **MOTHER**, *speaks directly to audience.)*

MOTHER. "...If you do not teach me, I shall not learn. If you do not love me, I shall not be loved...If I do not love you, I shall not love."

*(***MOTHER*** steps out of light. Hidden behind her, we now see* **DAUGHTER**, *13, small, frizzy-haired, adorable. She wears jeans, Lacoste polo-shirt, trendy sneakers; speaks directly to audience.)*

DAUGHTER. I came home from school, just like any other day. The kids had been teasing me all day about my new braces. Asshole Ricky Johnson, mostly...so, I was probably more cranky than usual. And I was probably gonna' tell her. Not definitely. I was always afraid she might try to do something when stuff like that happened...you know...maybe call Ricky's parents. Or Mrs. Goldstein, my teacher. She did that once, when Allen Woodbury kept pulling my bra-strap, and everybody found out about her calling Mrs. Goldstein...But, that's a whole other story.

(beat)

When I first found her, I'm pretty sure she was still breathing. I couldn't wake her. The fumes were wick'id, all over the house. It wasn't like she had left the stove on and burned a chicken or something like that. This was really different. This was definitely the car or some kind of engine smoke.

(beat)

I found her in the garage. She was inside the car and there was this hose taped to the exhaust pipe and then taped in through the window. She had taped this note to the car-window asking me to forgive her, telling me it wasn't about me, it was about her – telling me to leave her in the car and to call my father and that it wasn't my fault.

(beat)

I tried to get the car door open, but it was locked from the inside. I pulled the hose out of the window, and I broke the window open with one of my father's golf-clubs and I shut off the engine by turning the key. I opened the garage door and dragged her onto the driveway into fresh air, figuring that could help, but she was definitely dead by then. The doctors all said that she was definitely dead. I called 911, and then I called my father.

(beat)

It's only been a couple'a weeks, since it happened, so, I'm still pretty numb. I'll be okay, I guess.

(We hear now – **MOTHER'S VOICE**, *calling from the darkness, from another time.)*

MOTHER. Are you eating this food, or do I throw it away?

(Lights widen to include – Kitchen. Furnishings are Design-Within-Reach catalogue variety: Charles Eames chairs, Aalto table, etc.)

MOTHER. It's 10 o'clock! We should be going to bed at 10 o'clock, not starting dinner! We are not Spanish people!

(We hear – Sound of TV show, off-stage.)

DAUGHTER. *(from offstage)* It's just ending!

MOTHER. Now!

DAUGHTER. But, it's just ending!

MOTHER. Now!

(TV is turned off, sound ends. **DAUGHTER** *enters, now wears hoodie, different shoes.)*

DAUGHTER. It ended. It was dumb.

(looks at food)

What *is* that?

MOTHER. Dinner.
DAUGHTER. I know it's dinner, but, what is it?
MOTHER. Paella.

(**DAUGHTER** *laughs.*)

MOTHER. What's funny.
DAUGHTER. Paella's Spanish food.
MOTHER. Whatever. I ordered in.

(**DAUGHTER** *tries the food, hates it.*)

DAUGHTER. It's disgusting. Can I just have cereal?
MOTHER. Fine. Do want you want.

(**MOTHER** *takes plate from* **DAUGHTER***'s place at table, tosses it in trashcan.*)

DAUGHTER. You threw away the plate.
MOTHER. And the silverware.

(**MOTHER** *now tosses silverware in trashcan, as well.*)

DAUGHTER. I'm going to need a spoon.
MOTHER. There's one in the drawer.

(**DAUGHTER** *opens drawer, looks.*)

DAUGHTER. There are only two spoons left.
MOTHER. We're only two people. We only *need* two spoons.

(**DAUGHTER** *stands, finds cereal and milk, fills bowl. Returns to table.*)

DAUGHTER. Daddy called. Did you see my note?
MOTHER. I did. I saw it. An excellently communicated message.
DAUGHTER. Did you call him?
MOTHER. What would be the point of that?
DAUGHTER. I dunno. Maybe he wanted something.
MOTHER. That would be my guess.

(*beat*)

I talked to your father every day for eleven consecutive years. You have to draw the line, somewhere. How are your corn flakes?

DAUGHTER. Amazing.

MOTHER. I'm going to bed. Either wash your bowl or toss it. We have mice.

(Starts to exit. **DAUGHTER** *calls her, stopping her...)*

DAUGHTER. Mummy...?

MOTHER. What?

DAUGHTER. Nothing.

*(***MOTHER** *pauses, upstage-right.)*

MOTHER. My moods are not your responsibility. You don't cause them and you can't cure them. We are totally separate people. We are born alone and we die alone. You don't need anybody and nobody needs you. If I teach you anything at all, I will teach you that.

*(***DAUGHTER** *calls into darkness down-stage left.)*

DAUGHTER. Why'd you marry her, Daddy?

(Lights shifts from **MOTHER** *to* **FATHER**, *downstage-left. He answers, mid-conversation, from a different time.)*

FATHER. I married her because I loved her.

DAUGHTER. What does love feel like, Daddy?

FATHER. Like you need to be with the person, like you need to take care of the person.

DAUGHTER. I can see that.

FATHER. I love you. I feel those things for you.

DAUGHTER. But, not for Mummy?

FATHER. No. Not any more. No.

DAUGHTER. Because love stops?

FATHER. Sometimes.

(beat)

It's not easy to keep loving somebody if they don't love you back.

DAUGHTER. I can see that.

FATHER. I'll never stop loving you.

DAUGHTER. How do you know that, Daddy?

FATHER. Because I do. You're my daughter. That's the way it is.

DAUGHTER. How old were you when you started loving Mummy?

FATHER. Your age. 13. I had just moved here with my family. Grandpa had just started teaching at the Junior High. I was the new kid. Everybody knew my father was a teacher, so they treated me like I was a spy for the other side. Mummy sat behind me in geography and her mother had just died and I could tell how sad she was.

DAUGHTER. She must have been really sad.

FATHER. She was really really sad. That's when it started. She would cry, sometimes, without making any noise. Tears would just start coming out of her eyes. It had nothing to do with anything or anybody around her. I mean, she could be in French class, in the middle of conjugating the verb *avoir*. It happened a bunch of times, in front of the whole class. I would always ask her why, but she would never say anything specific. Then, one night, at supper, my father and mother were talking about this girl in our school and how her mother had committed suicide and how this girl had found her mother dead in their car in their garage and all...

*(Light restores on **MOTHER**, upstage.)*

MOTHER. ...There was this hose taped to the exhaust pipe and then taped in through the window. She had taped this note to the car-window asking me to forgive her, telling me it wasn't about me, it was about her – telling me to leave her in the car and to call my father and that it wasn't my fault...

DAUGHTER. *(to **FATHER**)* And you knew they were talking about Mummy?

FATHER. No doubt in my mind. I asked her if I could walk her home, next day, and I did, and on the way, I told her I knew what had happened, and she cried in my arms, and we've been together, ever since...well...you know what I mean.

MOTHER. I tried to get the car door open, but it was locked from the inside. I pulled the hose out of the window, and I broke the window open with one of my father's golf clubs and I shut off the engine by turning the key. I opened the garage door and dragged her onto the driveway into fresh air, figuring that could help, but she was definitely dead by then. The doctors all said that she was definitely dead. I called 911, and then I called my father.

DAUGHTER. Do you miss her?

MOTHER. I do. I miss her, every day.

FATHER. I do. But, mostly, I miss seeing you every day. That's what I miss most.

DAUGHTER. You don't love her anymore?

FATHER. No. Not like a husband. No.

DAUGHTER. I'm scared living here without you, Daddy. I'm scared she's going to do something.

FATHER. You could live with me. I'd love to have you live with me.

DAUGHTER. I can't, Daddy. I can't leave her alone.

*(We hear – sound of a single cello, hauntingly sad. Music will continue through end of play. Lights shift upstage to **MOTHER**, alone in tight light.)*

MOTHER. It's been 32 years, and I still can't begin to understand it. I can only feel its pull and it's so much more powerful than I can ever be, Emily. I can't fight it, anymore. You'll have to forgive me for this, Emily. This is not your doing, not your fault. This is not about you. This is about me. I am doing this for myself and only for myself. I cannot live with my sadness. My sadness is inconsolable. Forgive me. I love you. Mummy.

*(Light holds on **MOTHER**, as light restores on **FATHER**.)*

FATHER. It was like there were two of her, all the time… one who wanted to live, and one who most definitely did not want to live. They walked in parallel, side by side. My job seemed to be to guard the one of her who wanted to live from the other one – the inconsolable one. I know it was *her* choice, not about me. But, deep deep deep in this secret place in my soul, I will always wonder. The guilt I feel is boundless. And the anger I feel walks in precise parallel. How could she do what she did to our beautiful hopeful child?

(Lights cross to **DAUGHTER***, downstage. She is again dressed as she was at start of play: jeans, Lacoste polo-shirt, trendy sneakers.)*

DAUGHTER. I tried to get the car door open, but it was locked from the inside. I pulled the hose out of the window, and I broke the window open with one of my father's golf clubs and I shut off the engine by turning the key. I opened the garage door and dragged her onto the driveway into fresh air, figuring that could help, but she was definitely dead by then. The doctors all said that she was definitely dead. I called 911, and then I called my father.

(beat)

It's only been a couple'a weeks, since it happened, so, I'm still pretty numb. I'll be okay, I guess.

(We now hear – **MOTHER** *and* **DAUGHTER***'s voices, in unison, over loudspeakers, a soft whisper.)*

MOTHER & DAUGHTER *(V.O.)* "If you do not love me, I shall not be loved…If I do not love you, I shall not love."

MOTHER. "If you do not teach me, I shall not learn."

(Light fades out on **MOTHER***.)*

DAUGHTER. "If you do not teach me, I shall not learn."

(Light fades out on **DAUGHTER***.)*

(Music concludes.)

The Play is Over.

(12) NEW SHORTS

SPEAKING OF TUSHY

SPEAKING OF TUSHY had its 1st public reading at the Cherry Lane Theatre, NYC, June, 2007, presented by The New York Playwrights Lab, directed by Israel Horovitz.

Subsequently, the current draft of *SPEAKING OF TUSHY* was incorporated into a evening of short plays called *6 HOTELS*, which premiered at the Garson Theatre Center, Santa Fe, in June, 2008, directed by Israel Horovitz, with the following cast:

Stanley . . . . .Rod Harrison
Jean-Philippe . . . . .Joachin Torres
Stella . . . . .Jane May
Veronica . . . . .Marianna Bassha

THE PEOPLE OF THE PLAY

STANLEY - 30ish, American.
JEAN-PHILIPPE - 30ish, French.
STELLA - 30ish, American.
VERONICA - 30ish, English.

THE TIME OF THE PLAY

Scenes alternate between the present and flashbacks to the prior year.

THE PLACE OF THE PLAY

Action of the play alternates between two playing areas: a hotel room and a hotel bar.

A NOTE ON MUSIC

To differentiate between the two playing areas, when in hotel room, we should probably hear sound of a TV set at low volume. In bar, we should probably hear techno music or appropriately hip bar-music.

(Upstage, a hotel room with bed, dressing mirror. Downstage, bar and barstools.)

(Lights up on **STANLEY** *and* **JEAN-PHILIPPE***, at bar, drinking beer: Stella Artois.)*

STANLEY. You're French?

JEAN-PHILIPPE. From France.

STANLEY. You speak French?

JEAN-PHILIPPE. Uh…yuh, I do.

STANLEY. Jesus! Of *course*, you speak French! You're French. You're from there.

(and then…)

I'm not normally stupid. I'm depressed. Depression makes me stupid.

(and then…)

You live there or here?

JEAN-PHILIPPE. Here. I came here for college and stayed.

STANLEY. That's nice.

*(***JEAN-PHILLIPE** *lights a cigarette, inhales, remembers he has quit smoking, puts it out. Tosses cigarette packette to* **STANLEY.***)*

JEAN-PHILIPPE. Here's a gift. I quit smoking, six weeks ago.

*(***STANLEY** *puts packette in pocket.)*

STANLEY. Yuh, me, too. Friend's mother died from smoking.

JEAN-PHILIPPE. Just been through that. Smoking's a terrible addiction.

STANLEY. I know.

(And then…)

I'm so depressed.

JEAN-PHILIPPE. A woman?

STANLEY. A very complicated woman. She hurt me.

JEAN-PHILIPPE. *(nods, sympathetically)* They do that.

STANLEY. I mean she *really* hurt me.

JEAN-PHILIPPE. They really do that.

STANLEY. I know I'm better off without her.

JEAN-PHILIPPE. Possibly better off without *any* of them.

STANLEY. She thinks her ass is fat.

JEAN-PHILIPPE. They all do.

   (STELLA calls downstage to STANLEY.)

STELLA. Does this dress make me look fat, Stanley?

   (Lights shift to – hotel room, upstage. We meet – STELLA, not fat, not skinny.)

STELLA. Stan?

   (No response.)

   Did you hear me, Stanley?

STANLEY. *(moving upstage into hotel room)* Of course, I heard you.

STELLA. So, are you, like, embarrassed to answer me?

STANLEY. Why would I be embarrassed to answer you?

STELLA. I hate this dress!

   (She rips off dress, opens large suitcase, rummages through other clothing.)

   I hate everything in this suitcase!

   (and then...)

   You'll have to go without me.

STANLEY. Are you *kidding*?

STELLA. No.

STANLEY. It's your mother's funeral. How the hell am I supposed to go to your mother's funeral without you? I'm supposed to explain to your family that your dress made your ass look fat?

   (STELLA lights a cigarette.)

STANLEY. Hey! What are you doing? Put it out!

STELLA. I want to smoke.

STANLEY. Fine. Smoke.

STELLA. You think my ass is fat, don't you?

STANLEY. Stella! I don't! I DON'T think that!

STELLA. It's so embarrassing. People look at me, that's what they think: fat ass.

STANLEY. Stella, for God's sake, stop it! Your ass is not fat!

STELLA. It's not thin!…Can you look me straight in the eye and tell me, honestly, that my ass is thin? Can you do that?

(She checks her bottom in mirror.)

Is my daisy fading?

STANLEY. It looks like it always looks.

STELLA. Why are you staring at my ass?

STANLEY. I'm not. I'm checking your daisy.

STELLA. You are! You think my ass is fat, don't you, Stanley? *(a possible "Streetcar" moment)* …*STANLEY!*

*(**STANLEY** rolls his eyes to Heaven, calls downstage to **JEAN-PHILIPPE**.)*

STANLEY. *(while moving to bar, downstage…)* The amazing thing is how much I miss her. Of course, I miss *high school*, and that was also a nightmare.

JEAN-PHILIPPE. You shouldn't miss this woman. She hurt you. You should be happy to be free of her.

STANLEY. You're right. It was a misery in the end.

(beat)

It was a misery in the middle, too.

(beat)

It started well.

(beat)

Actually…not that well.

*(**STELLA** calls to **STANLEY** from end of bar, as **JEAN-PHILIPPE** exits.)*

STELLA. Why'd your parents pick 'Stanley'? Stanley's kind of a nothing name. Why'd they pick it?

(**STANLEY** *joins* **STELLA**.)

STANLEY. I dunno. I never asked them. I just sort of *accepted* it. They'd yell 'Stanley', I'd yell 'What do you want"?… And we just kept going.

(and then…)

Your name is…?

STELLA. Stella.

STANLEY. Streetcar?

STELLA. No, Stella. Why the would you think my parents named me *Streetcar*?

STANLEY. You're Stella, I'm Stanley…Streetcar? Brando?

STELLA. Brando what? What are you talking about?

STANLEY. The movie. *Streetcar Named Desire.*

STELLA. What about it?

STANLEY. I…nothing. Stella's a lovely name. I like it.

STELLA. It means 'pot roast' in Italian.

STANLEY. Are you sure about that?

STELLA. Positive. My parents told me.

STANLEY. Okay.

(smiles)

I wish my parents had named me Stella instead of Stanley.

STELLA. You're kidding.

STANLEY. Uh, yuh. I am.

STELLA. See that? I *thought* you were kidding. People would laugh at you if your name was Stella. Stella's a girl's name.

STANLEY. Uh, yes, it is. Stella is a girl's name.

(Suddenly, the sound of **VERONICA** *imitating a bell.)*

VERONICA. DING DING DING!

(**VERONICA** *enters. She's pretty, English, speaks with a pronounced South London accent.*)

VERONICA. Brilliant, Stella! Totally brilliant! You definitely win!

STANLEY. Uh, what's going on?

VERONICA. We're having a Dumb-Off, and Stella's just scored off the bloody charts!

STANLEY. Excuse me?

VERONICA. A Dumb-Off. You walk up to a strange bloke at a bar. You've got thirty seconds to be dumber than Marmite. Dumb buys Dumber's drink.

(to **STELLA***)*

Absolutely brill, Stella! What are you drinking?

STELLA. Vodka gimlet.

VERONICA. *(to* **STANLEY***)* You?

STANLEY. Me? I'm okay, thanks.

VERONICA. Oh, no, you get a drink on me. That's the deal.

STANLEY. Okay. Sweet. I'll have whatever Dumb-Dumb's having.

VERONICA. Vodka gimlet.

STANLEY. Ok. That. I'll have that.

VERONICA. *(calls upstage to imagined bartender)* Two vodka gimlets, please, Francesca.

STANLEY. No, wait! I'll have a fresh Stella. *(calls out in a Stanley Kowalski voice)* STELLL-AAAAA!

*(***STELLA** *and* **VERONICA** *exchange an OMG! glance.* **STANLEY** *sees it.)*

STANLEY. I guess that's not new to you.

STELLA. Not new.

VERONICA. Change that to on vodka gimlet and one Stella, please, Francesca. I'm going to the loo. *(exits)*

STANLEY. So. That's amazing! You're not dumb?

STELLA. Not dumb.

STANLEY. You're really not dumb? You were playing with me?

STELLA. I was, Stanley. Sorry.

STANLEY. You're *really* not dumb? You know who Brando is?

STELLA. Brando – Stanley...Stella – Kim Hunter...Blanche – Vivien Leigh...Director – Kazan...And for ten bonus points, who wrote the screenplay?

STANLEY. The screenplay for 'Streetcar'?...Uh, Tenessee Williams?

STELLA. BZZZZ! Incorrect! Screenplay was written by Oscar Saul, based on Williams' play.

STANLEY. I'm impressed.

STELLA. Film Studies major, Hampshire College...M.A., Columbia Film School...

STANLEY. Wow! You went to Hampshire?

STELLA. That was a while ago. I shave my legs, now.

STANLEY. I went to UMass-Amherst, undergrad and grad. Doctorate in Political Science, which is basically preparation for collecting unemployment. I teach junior high school English in Bushwick.

STELLA. You want to share a room, upstairs? I get a corporate rate.

STANLEY. *(an astonished pause, and then...)* Sure.

(JEAN-PHILIPPE crosses downstage to STANLEY. STELLA exits upstage.)

JEAN-PHILIPPE. Do I come to this hotel a lot? I suppose I do. I used to come here really a lot...with my girlfriend.

STANLEY. Me, too. Here. With my girlfriend. Now, I just come here alone.

JEAN-PHILIPPE. Me, too.

STANLEY. Painful.

JEAN-PHILIPPE. Painful.

STANLEY. Makes me really depressed.

JEAN-PHILIPPE. Me, too.

STANLEY. Why do you think you do it?

JEAN-PHILIPPE. Come here?

STANLEY. Yuh, why?

JEAN-PHILIPPE. Because I'm a *chien-malade.*

STANLEY. Sorry. I took Russian.

JEAN-PHILIPPE. *Chien-malade* means sick puppy.

(and then...)

Every hotel is haunted by a million memories...most of them painful.

(Lights cross to **STELLA***, in hotel room, upstage. She calls into bathroom.)*

STELLA. Are you never coming out of there!?... That is the longest shower in history!...You weren't that dirty! Trust me!

(JEAN-PHILIPPE*, enters from bathroom, toweling his hair.)*

JEAN-PHILIPPE. I love showers. I love rain. I love the Brooklyn Bridge. I love Pastis. I love *boeuf tartar.* I love Serge Gainsbourg. And I love you, *mon amour.*

(He leans in to kiss **STELLA.** *She pulls back from him.)*

STELLA. We have to stop.

JEAN-PHILIPPE. Stop what?

STELLA. Seeing each other.

JEAN-PHILIPPE. *Why?*

STELLA. I've had enough.

JEAN-PHILIPPE. You've had enough *what?* What does "I've had enough" *mean*, Stella?

STELLA. I've had enough means I've had enough. This isn't a positive thing for me, anymore, J-P. The French accent was a turn-on for a couple'a weeks, but, time's up, Froggie.

JEAN-PHILIPPE. Are you *kidding?* I...I...

STELLA. Come onnn! Don't play wounded. It's time to move on.

JEAN-PHILIPPE. I...Are you *kidding?*

STELLA. I need to clear my life out, get the numbers down.

(Checks herself in mirror...)

Does my ass look fat?

JEAN-PHILIPPE. Wait a minute! Wait a minute! Wait a minute!…Get *what* numbers down? Are you saying there's somebody else?

STELLA. Of course, there's somebody else! There's always somebody else! He's gonna' take a walk, too. I'm bored. I need fresh inventory.

JEAN-PHILIPPE. Jesus, Stella! Are you talking about people, or *clutter*!?

STELLA. What's the difference?

(Throws two $100 bills on to the bed.)

There's my share of the room.

JEAN-PHILIPPE. Jesus, Stella! I mean…what the fuck kind of monster are you?

STELLA. I know. It's, like, a huge shock, isn't it? Men never expect women to act like men.

*(Lights crossfade to **STANLEY**, at bar, drunk.)*

STANLEY. Why can't we fall in love with women who love us? I never have. I always love women who don't love me.

(Beat.)

I don't think my mother loved me. She never said she did. My grandmother hated me. They both loved my brother Arnold. He designs outsize dresses in Nevada. Don't ask.

JEAN-PHILIPPE. *(Crosses to bar, also drunk.)* Did you ever see this Starbucks White Cup?

(Takes crushed Starbucks coffee cup from pocket, reads from it.)

"You simply can't make someone love you if they don't. You must choose someone who already loves you. If you choose someone who does not love you, this is the kind of love you must want."

STANLEY. That is so depressing.

JEAN-PHILIPPE. Oui. I know. It's become my mantra.

STANLEY. You carry that in your pocket?

JEAN-PHILIPPE. I do.

STANLEY. That is really sad.

JEAN-PHILIPPE. It could be worse.

STANLEY. "There's nothing so bad that it can't grow worse There's no limit to how bad things can be." Beckett.

JEAN-PHILIPPE. "We know sad, so that we can recognize happy. All our experience is relative. We know bad so we can recognize good, loss so we can know what we've had. Jean-Paul Sartre.

STANLEY. We know bad so that we can recognize worse. We know disaster so that we can recognize catastrophe.

JEAN-PHILIPPE. Who said that?

(A drunken, confused pause. And then...)

STANLEY. Me. Stanley.

JEAN-PHILIPPE. You're not a happy man.

STANLEY. No one in my family has ever been happy. Not since the Old Testament.

JEAN-PHILIPPE. How do you deal with your sadness?

STANLEY. I drink. I complain. I cry. And you? How do you deal with your sadness?

JEAN-PHILIPPE. New women. I try to meet many many new women. It helps. *Je suis Français.*

(JEAN-PHILLIPE calls to VERONICA at opposite end of bar.)

JEAN-PHILIPPE. Where were you born, Veronica?

(VERONICA moves downstage to JEAN-PHILIPPE. STANLEY exits upstage.)

VERONICA. South London. A leafy village aptly named Dulwich.

JEAN-PHILIPPE. Because it's dull.

VERONICA. Because it's dull. Sorry, what's your name? Philippe-something.

JEAN-PHILIPPE. Jean-Philippe.

VERONICA. Jean-Philippe. Jean-Philippe. Jean-Philippe. Cool. I wish my parents named *me* Jean-Philippe.

JEAN-PHILIPPE. I wish they had, as well. And I wish my parents had named me Veronica.

VERONICA. Why do you wish that?

JEAN-PHILIPPE. Because, then, we would be a couple named Jean-Philippe and Veronica. And that would be lovely.

VERONICA. Lovely.

(They stare at each other for a moment, smiling, wordlessly.)

VERONICA. Your eyes are the color of swimming pools. Are you wearing tinted lenses?

JEAN-PHILIPPE. No, my father was a swimming pool.

VERONICA. Your biological father.

JEAN-PHILIPPE. My biological father.

VERONICA. I never met a funny Frenchman, before. You're unusual.

JEAN-PHILIPPE. That's why they made me leave the country. I was too funny.

(and then...)

Your friend does a great dumb-down. I was totally fooled.

VERONICA. Stella does *the* most brilliant dumb-down. I *love* her! We did a Dumb-Off at Tribeca Grille, last night… This French bloke is, like, totally astonished by her stupidity, holds up three fingers, asks "How many fingers am I holding up?", and Stella goes "Uhhhh, is this a trick question?"

JEAN-PHILIPPE. Whoa! Noooo! That was *me*! Ten minutes ago!

(VERONICA smiles. JEAN-PHILIPPE realizes.)

JEAN-PHILIPPE. Oh. Ohhhhhhh.

(He laughs.)

You're an unusual woman, Veronica.

VERONICA. Would you like to have sex with me?

JEAN-PHILIPPE. I couldn't. I have too much respect for you.

VERONICA. Get over it.

(VERONICA leans in for a kiss. As soon as their lips touch, lights shift downstage. JEAN-PHILIPPE turns, as STANLEY calls to him. VERONICA exits to hotel room.)

STANLEY. Oh, my god! That is fantastic!

JEAN-PHILIPPE. I was completely, utterly off-guard.

STANLEY. I can imagine.

> *(beat)*
>
> So, did you, ya' know, like…?

JEAN-PHILIPPE. I had very little choice.

STANLEY. I see that.

> *(and then…)*
>
> Can I ask you something personal?

JEAN-PHILIPPE. Shoot.

STANLEY. What's your average for a week?

JEAN-PHILIPPE. My average for…?

STANLEY. Well, uh, doing it.

JEAN-PHILIPPE. Ah. Doing it. Then or now?

STANLEY. Now. Recent.

JEAN-PHILIPPE. Let's say ten-to-thirteen.

STANLEY. Times a week?! *Average?*

JEAN-PHILIPPE. My ex-girlfriend was highly charged…

STANLEY. My best week was three. I'm pathetic.

JEAN-PHILIPPE. Three's not terrible.

STANLEY. Three's *terrible*. And that was my best week, *ever*!

> *(and then…)*
>
> Whoa! That just triggered the worst possible memory.

(Lights shift to **VERONICA**, *in hotel room)*

VERONICA. I need to use the bathroom! Hello in there! Are you ever going to let me use the bathroom?!…

*(**STANLEY** enters from bathroom, toweling his hair.)*

STANLEY. Sorry. It's all yours.

VERONICA. Were you *masturbating* in there?

STANLEY. *What?*

VERONICA. Were you *masturbating* in there? I thought something was happening in there, 'cause nothing ever happened out here, did it?

STANLEY. Am I hearing you correctly? Did you actually say what I *think* you just said?

VERONICA. You heard me.

STANLEY. Jesus, Veronica! This isn't so easy for me, you know? I'm not a cheater.

VERONICA. Excuse me?

STANLEY. I'm not a cheater. This doesn't sit...

VERONICA. Excuse me? Am I hearing what I *think* I'm hearing?

STANLEY. I thought Stella was your friend.

VERONICA. Stella's my *closest* friend.

STANLEY. So, why'd you trick me into coming here? Why'd you make me think Stella was meeting me here? Why?

VERONICA. I have no intention of listening to a middle-class morals lecture, thank you very much.

STANLEY. You don't feel guilty?

VERONICA. Not in the slightest.

STANLEY. Well...you're...unusual.

VERONICA. Ever try fucking yourself?

STANLEY. It'd be more interesting than fucking *you*, doll-face.

VERONICA. Do you leave, quietly, or do I call the police, you pathetic fucking non-fuck?

STANLEY. Happy to leave.

VERONICA. You don't think Stella is faithful to you, do you?

STANLEY. I...yuh, yes...I do.

VERONICA. You can't be *serious*?

STANLEY. I...I...Are you the worst English person, ever, or is the whole of England just basically shitty people?

(Lights cross to **JEAN-PHILIPPE** *at bar.* **STANLEY** *calls to him.)*

STANLEY. Have you ever hit a woman?

*(***STANLEY** *joins* **JEAN-PHILIPPE** *at bar. They are seriously drunk, on their way to dangerously drunk.)*

JEAN-PHILIPPE. With my hand?

STANLEY. Hand, or stick.

JEAN-PHILIPPE. I haven't. Have you?

STANLEY. No. Have you?

JEAN-PHILIPPE. No. Have you?

STANLEY. No. Have you?

JEAN-PHILIPPE. No. Have you?

STANLEY. No. Have you?

JEAN-PHILIPPE. No. Have you?

STANLEY. No. I couldn't. I hope I can, some day…I've *been* hit.

JEAN-PHILIPPE. By a woman?

STANLEY. Women. Plural. Many.

JEAN-PHILIPPE. I'm impressed. Hand or stick?

STANLEY. Hand, definitely. There was possibly a stick involved.

(beat)

When I was younger, I was really annoying.

(beat)

I grew up into a really annoying adult.

(and then…)

I am very very drunk. What is Pastis made from, anyway?

JEAN-PHILIPPE. Pastis is made from more Pastis.

(Somehow, saying this has made **JEAN-PHILIPPE** *laugh, really cracked him up.)*

JEAN-PHILIPPE. Oh, God.

STANLEY. What?

JEAN-PHILIPPE. Usually, when I'm very very very drunk, like I am at this moment, and I laugh, like now, I vomit.

STANLEY. Really? That's funny.

JEAN-PHILIPPE. *(sudden change of mood)* I cannot stop asking myself what this other man had that I need.

STANLEY. You still love her, don't you?

JEAN-PHILIPPE. She has this tattoo.

STANLEY. I know. On her tushy.

JEAN-PHILIPPE. This little daisy.

STANLEY. This little green and yellow daisy.

JEAN-PHILIPPE. A daisy *daisy*! Daisies are *daisy*.

(Begins to laugh, again.)

Oh, God.

STANLEY. What?

JEAN-PHILIPPE. *(chortling)* Pastis is *Pastis*.

(Now, full laughter. And then…)

Oh, God.

STANLEY. Are you going to vomit?

JEAN-PHILIPPE. *(still laughing)* I am!

STANLEY. Your girlfriend really has a daisey on her tushy?

JEAN-PHILIPPE. She does *(and then…)* Oo-la-la! Attends!

STANLEY AND JEAN-PHILIPPE. Your girlfriend has a daisy on her tushy?!

(They realize, slap their own foreheads, in unison. And then, they turn from one another and both scream, in unison, three screams – primal, animal-like, absolute Kowalski…)

STANLEY AND JEAN-PHILIPPE. *STELLA! STELLA! STELLLLLAAAAA!*

(They turn, stare at each other, helplessly…)

(The lights fade to black.)

The Play is Over.

2ND VIOLIN

2ND VIOLIN had its world premiere on June 7, 2008, at the Garson Theatre, Santa Fe, New Mexico, in *6 Hotels*, directed by Israel Horovitz with the following cast:

Evvie	Jane May
Catherine	Marianna Bassham
Marvin	Rod Harrison
Sergei	Joaquin Torres

THE PEOPLE OF THE PLAY

EVVIE - 30ish, dark-haired, beautiful.
CATHERINE - 30ish, blonde, beautiful.
MARVIN - 40ish, short, husky.
SERGEI - 60ish, silver-haired, Slavic, smarmy.

THE TIME OF THE PLAY

Night. The present.

THE PLACE OF THE PLAY

Hotel room adjacent to hotel's ballroom.

NOTE
The actors should mime playing, using actual instruments, but no bow.

(In darkness, we hear – symphony orchestra playing Strauss symphony Ein Heldenleben. *Orchestra fades out and we are left with sound of violinist practicing violin solo from* Ein Heldenleben. *After a few moments of pristine playing, we hear a small mistake. And then, a larger mistake. And then...)*

EVVIE. Shit piss motherfucker!

(Lights fade up in hotel room.)

(We meet the violinist **EVVIE**, *30, dark-haired, slim, beautiful.* **EVVIE** *holds violin under her chin, sits in chair opposite* **CATHERINE**, *a cellist.* **CATHERINE** *is blonde, slightly older than* **EVVIE**, *a tad chubby.)*

*(***CATHERINE** *is in midst of changing from street clothes into a black dress, sensible shoes.* **EVVIE** *wears a bathrobe. A black dress [like* **CATHERINE***'s dress] hangs on clothes-rack behind her.)*

CATHERINE. That was fine.

EVVIE. That was not fine.

CATHERINE. Evvie, that was fine.

EVVIE. That was not fine, Catherine!

*(***CATHERINE** *is now in her underwear. Suddenly, door opens, assistant orchestra manager [***MARVIN***] pokes his head into room.)*

MARVIN. Fifteen minutes, ladies.

CATHERINE. Thanks, Marv. Nice.

MARVIN. Sorry.

*(***CATHERINE** *pulls her dress over her head.)*

EVVIE. Thanks, Marv.

MARV. *(and then, to* **EVVIE***)* You need anything, Evvie? Spring-water? Rapid backstage sex?

EVVIE. I'll take a rain-check, Marv.

MARV. *(amazed and hopeful)* Really?

EVVIE. The spring-water, Marv.

CATHERINE. Get out of here, Marv.

MARV. You'll be great, Ev.

EVVIE. Thanks, Marv.

CATHERINE. Out!

(**MARVIN** *exits.*)

EVVIE. It's not fine, Catherine. Sergei has me playing these 32 bars to open *Ein Heldenleben*. He's rewriting Richard Strauss. He's a lunatic. Single violin. Me. Just me. If I make the same mistakes in fifteen minutes, in front of the audience, are you going to think it was fine?…

CATHERINE. Try it again.

EVVIE. …Or are you going to think it sucked?

CATHERINE. Sucked. But, you're not going to do that on stage. Try it again.

EVVIE. Couldn't somebody have told me last night the diva-bitch was sick?! I could have practiced all day today. I could have had something.

CATHERINE. You have something, already. You'll have something even better in fifteen minutes.

EVVIE. Fourteen minutes.

CATHERINE. Fourteen minutes. Try it again.

(**EVVIE** *plays the same refrain, gets to the same place, makes the same mistakes, has the same reaction.*)

EVVIE. Shit piss motherfucker!

CATHERINE. Okay, okay, work it with me. Now.

(**CATHERINE** *readies her cello.*)

One two three four…

(**CATHERINE** *nods, bows her cello.* **EVVIE** *bows her violin. They play in sweet harmony until the same refrain, same mistakes occur.*)

CATHERINE. Okay, we have a problem. Let's break it down.

(**CATHERINE** *plays cello and talks at same time.*)

CATHERINE. Play the first note strong and clear, ok?...Then make sure the triplets are even. DON'T rush these sixteenths coming up. Put some weight into the accents... and then give yourself time for the shift. Now, HERE, the notes are accented, but they still have to sing, use more speed and vibrate. A-flat, G-flat, F-flat, E-flat...

(*Now,* **EVVIE** *plays and talks through the changes, slowly, clearly, perfectly...*)

EVVIE. A-flat, G-flat, F-flat, E-flat...A-flat, G-flat, F-flat, E-flat...

CATHERINE. A-flat, G-flat, F-flat, E-flat...

(**EVVIE** *plays, tentatively.*)

CATHERINE. (*Still playing and talking.*) Ok, good, better!... In the next phrase, make sure your left hand is ahead of the string crossings. And this part even more confidently ... and then a big crescendo.

(**EVVIE** *plays. Tentatively.*)

CATHERINE. You're not feeling the big picture, Ev. You'll never fly through it, later, unless you nail it slow, now.

(**EVVIE** *plays, tentatively.*)

EVVIE. (*as she plays*) I can nail it slow! That's not the problem.

(*completes the solo*)

Okay? Was that better?

CATHERINE. Much better, see?...Now, at speed. Keep the pulse going the whole time, DON'T rush.

(**CATHERINE** *nods, bows her cello.* **EVVIE** *bows her violin. They play the same refrain in sweet harmony until the same mistake occurs.*)

EVVIE. Shoot me! Somebody fuckin' shoot me!

(*and then...*)

I want to go home. I want to be under my bed with my

cat.

CATHERINE. Stop it! You're being ridiculous! This is all happening in your head. You've played this piece a hundred times.

EVVIE. Not the solo. Never the solo. I'm a second chair, Catherine. That's who I am. I'm not a soloist. I can't do this.

CATHERINE. Yuh, well, *I'm* a second chair and I would KILL for the chance you're getting.

EVVIE. That's ridiculous! You could get first chair, any time you want, and you know it! You're a million times more talented than Pussyface. You know you are, Catherine!

CATHERINE. I don't want to talk about it.

EVVIE. Oh oh oh! Wait wait wait! You don't want to TALK ABOUT IT and I'm stepping out on stage in...*(looks at watch)*...12 minutes and I'm going to be FINE?! Is there not some inequality here in what is open for discussion? I am about to play Strauss's masterpiece *Ein Heldenleben* backwards, for a certifiable lunatic who thinks he knows more than Richard Strauss! I...

(A knock at the door. **CATHERINE** *and* **EVVIE** *look up.* **SERGEI** *calls from off-stage.)*

SERGEI. Are you decent?

*(***CATHERINE** *and* **EVVIE** *exchange a worried glance.)*

EVVIE. Could he hear me?

CATHERINE. I don't know.

(her sweetest voice:)

Come in, Sergei.

*(***SERGEI** *enters. He is a Herbert von Karajan wannabe, suave, grey-haired, speaks with Russian accent, wears white tie and tails, carries baton and sheet music.)*

SERGEI. *(to* **EVVIE***)* I've come to see my new star. Oh, my God! Your hair, Evelyn!...

EVVIE. What? What's wrong?

SERGEI. Oh, my God! I love it!

EVVIE. You do? I, well, I...thank you.

SERGEI. Oh, my God! That color! It's beautiful, that color! What did call that color?

EVVIE. Brown.

SERGEI. Brown. I love it!

(sees her dress on clothes-rack)

Your dress is *glorious*! Is that a new design?

EVVIE. No...Well, new*ish*. H&M. I, uh...

(doesn't finish thought)

SERGEI. This will be a magnificent night for both of us.

EVVIE. I, uh...Yuh, well. I...There could be...

SERGEI. I love change. Change is opportunity. I have conducted *Ein Heldenleben* a dozen times and it's always been brilliant, but, tonight...? *(shrugs)* Tonight...?

*(There is a small silence, which **EVVIE** cannot bear.)*

EVVIE. What?

SERGEI. Tonight, I predict *magnificence*! Tonight, *Ein Heldenleben* will finally be in a structure that truly makes it a masterpiece. Richard Strauss will look down from the pantheon and he will be amazed that, finally, finally, *Ein Heldenleben* has been *realized*!...Evelyn, do you know what *Ein Heldenleben* means in English?

EVVIE. No...Well, not exactly..."A heroic life"?

SERGEI. No, no! A *hero's* life! And you will be the hero, tonight, Evelyn.

EVVIE. I, uh...Yuh, well. I...There could be a problem, Sergei. I...

SERGEI. No, I had it wrong. *I* will be the hero, and you will be my heroine, Evelyn. Oh, my God! Look at you! You are *radiant*!

*(**SERGEI** kisses **EVVIE** on the lips. And then...)*

SERGEI. There will be an orchestra and there will be an auditorium filled with a thousand influential people, but, for me, Evelyn, there will be you and me – Sergei and Evelyn – and nobody else. Oh, my God, I love the color of your hair! And those eyes! Look at them looking at me! I love them!

(SERGEI kisses EVVIE on the lips, again. And then, he exits. There is a small astonished pause, and then...)

EVVIE. What just happened?

What just happened?

What the hell just happened?!

CATHERINE. What happened is that pompous Russian Eurotrash prick did not say hello to me. He walked in, he walked out, and I would have gotten more human contact from him if I was the *doorknob*!

EVVIE. He just kissed me on the lips, yes? He did this. I didn't hallucinate this. This happened, yes? *Answer me!*

CATHERINE. He needs you.

EVVIE. He does?

CATHERINE. You go out there and mess up, how does he look?

EVVIE. Bad. He looks bad.

CATHERINE. Exactly.

EVVIE. *THAT IS SO MUCH PRESSURE!*

CATHERINE. You'll be fine.

EVVIE. *STOP SAYING THAT!*

(MARVIN pokes his head in the door.)

MARVIN. Ten minutes, ladies!

(To EVVIE, who sees MARVIN looking at her breasts, pulls her loose robe closed.)

Sergei's really pumped about this. He's really excited. He told Edgar he was really excited.

CATHERINE. C'mon, Marv, Sergei's always excited. Sergei gets excited when he swipes his Metro card.

MARVIN. I guess.

(to EVVIE)

You ready for this, Ev?

CATHERINE. She's ready, Marv.

MARVIN. I'm kind've pumped myself. It's exciting when a #2 moves up.

CATHERINE. How long have you been an assistant orchestra manager, Marv?

MARVIN. Me?

CATHERINE. Uh, yuh, you.

MARVIN. 16 years, as of November. 10 years, here, under Edgar.

CATHERINE. Does it excite you to be playing a fundraiser in a hotel ballroom?

MARVIN. Well, no, it doesn't excite me, but the orchestra does need the money.

CATHERINE. This orchestra needs more than money, Marv. Let me ask you something…Who's a better orchestra manager? You or Edgar?

MARVIN. Jees, Catherine…Don't make me answer that.

CATHERINE. Ever run a concert on your own?

MARVIN. When Edgar's out sick kind of thing?

CATHERINE. Yuh.

MARVIN. Well, yuh, sure, maybe a half dozen times over the years. He doesn't really ever let himself get sick on performance days. I mean, he has to be almost dying. Half a dozen times in 10 years, maybe.

CATHERINE. How'd you like it?

MARVIN. Running the show on my own?

(beat)

I liked it.

(beat)

Made me nervous. Edgar took two days off, when his mother died…I knew in advance I'd be running three performances on my own – two nights and a matinee. I couldn't sleep, got the shakes.

(smiles)

I get nervous.

(burps)

Excuse me. That was gross. I ate some kind of weird shrubbery from the hotel restaurant. Health food. Made me gassy.

(and then)

That was your ten.

(**MARVIN** *exits. There is a small pause. And then...*)

CATHERINE. You have to do this. You've got the skills. You know the piece.

EVVIE. My hands are freezing cold. Feel them.

(**EVVIE** *offers her hands to* **CATHERINE**, *who takes them, holds them.*)

CATHERINE. They're freezing cold.

EVVIE. That's what I just told you.

CATHERINE. It's hot in here.

EVVIE. I know. I'm really scared.

CATHERINE. You know the piece. The problem's not the music. The problem's between your ears. Work it through with me, slowly.

(**CATHERINE** *nods, bows her cello, plays and talks at same time.*)

CATHERINE. *(as she plays)* Start here, like, *decisively*, and confidently ... crescendo to the peak of the phrase...

(**EVVIE** *takes three deep breaths.*)

EVVIE. I can do this, I can do this, I can do this. A-flat, G-flat, F-flat, E-flat, resolve...

(She bows her violin, plays and talks through the changes, slowly, clearly, perfectly.)

EVVIE. ...Confidently...crescendo.

CATHERINE. Don't rush it...increase intensity...don't give away too much, not even here. This is what Sergei's looking for, whether he knows it or not.

(**CATHERINE** *and* **EVVIE** *play in unison until the same refrain, the same mistakes occur.*)

CATHERINE. No!

EVVIE. It is the Bermuda fucking triangle!

(and then...)

I know it's in my head!
I know it's in my head!
I know it's in my head!

(and then...)

I am totally screwed.

CATHERINE. You'll be fine.

EVVIE. *(screams)* STOP TELLING ME THAT, CATHERINE!

(Beat. And then...)

Sorry. I'm sorry. I'm sorry.

(There is a small silence. **CATHERINE** *speaks first, sadly.)*

CATHERINE. I covered first chair for Alex, when his wife had the baby.

EVVIE. I...I remember. I...I was there.

CATHERINE. Shostakovich's first Cello Concerto. I totally choked. I so blew up the cadenza.

EVVIE. You did fine.

(and then...)

I can't believe I just said that. I'm sorry.

(and then...)

Most of it was good. You got through the first two movements, perfectly. The fourth movement was good, too. It's a really tough cadenza...polyphonic...the cello writing is totally tortured. You were nervous and...

CATHERINE. *(cuts her off)* Please, don't! I was totally *prepared*. I had a week with a coach. I played that cadenza, brilliantly, fifty times in two days before the concert. I totally choked. My palms were so soaked with sweat, I could barely hold the bow. No wonder Sergei doesn't look at me. *WHAT IS THE MATTER WITH US?!*

(There is a substantial pause.)

EVVIE. I think soloists may be, like, different from us, Catherine.

CATHERINE. *I'm not like you! I'm nothing like you!*

(There is a small silence.)

EVVIE. Okay.

CATHERINE. I'm sorry. I'm really sorry. That came out so totally wrong. I've been playing cello since I was 6 years old. I was never a kid like other kids were kids. You know what I'm saying?

EVVIE. 'Course I do.

CATHERINE. This is all my parents ever wanted from me.

EVVIE. Me, too. Same deal.

(and then...)

My father played violin in our community orchestra. He was terrible. He taught math in junior high. I mean, that's what he really did...but, in his dreams, this is what he did...violin. He loved violin. This is what he wanted for me, sooo much. He cried when I got into Oberlin. Even with my half-scholarship, it was still so expensive he had to take a 2nd job...He worked nights at Stop'n'shop, stocking produce.

(and then...)

How could I ever not do this?

(There is a small silence. And then, rather than weep, **CATHERINE** *bows her cello. The resultant sound is all sadness, agonized.)*

*(***EVVIE*** bows her violin, joins in. The duet is deeply emotional, all improvised, spontaneous. They continue to play for half a minute.)*

(When they stop playing, They look at each other, lovingly. Both are weeping, their faces tear-stained.)

*(***MARVIN*** knocks, opens the door, pokes his head inside.)*

MARVIN. What was that? That was so beautiful.

(Sees they're upset.)

You okay?

CATHERINE. We're fine, Marv.

EVVIE. We're okay.

MARVIN. That was beautiful. Whose piece is that?

EVVIE. Catherine's.

CATHERINE. Evvie's.

EVVIE. We wrote it together.

MARVIN. It's beautiful. It's so sad.

CATHERINE. Are we at five, Marv?

MARVIN. What? Oh. Yes. This is your five minute call, ladies.

CATHERINE. Thanks, Marv.

EVVIE. Thanks, Marv.

MARVIN. You're gonna be great, Ev. I know you are. I've got a definitely positive feeling on this. You're going to be amazing.

EVVIE. I…Thank you, Marv.

*(**MARVIN** exits.)*

CATHERINE. That man is such a loser.

EVVIE. That's really harsh. I like Marvin. He's nice.

CATHERINE. He gives me the creeps.

EVVIE. A little creepy, but he means well.

(And then, as she tunes violin…)

I've got a sticky peg.

CATHERINE. How many times in the last year has he opened the dressing room door and walked in on you while you were changing?

EVVIE. Several.

CATHERINE. And how many of these times were you down to underwear or less?

EVVIE. Several.

CATHERINE. You think that's just a happy accident?

EVVIE. I never thought about it.

CATHERINE. Marv's a keyholer.

EVVIE. Marv's gay, Catherine.

CATHERINE. Not!

EVVIE. Really?

CATHERINE. He tries to pass as gay. He's not. Trust me.

EVVIE. Really!?

CATHERINE. Lonely, insecure women are easy prey for lonely, insecure men like Marv. They ask, nicely, night after night, and, eventually, you say, "What the hell". Beats sitting alone watching *Sex In The City* DVDs on my iMac."

EVVIE. You slept with Marv?

CATHERINE. I was awake with Marv, which was much worse. Trust me.

(And then, as she bows cello, turning pegs, tuning cello.)

Jesus, I'm getting a wolftone. Hear it?

EVVIE. Sounds fine to me.

CATHERINE. This fuzzy, weird sound…It's getting better.

EVVIE. Why am I so scared? I've done nothing with my entire life but get ready for this!

CATHERINE. There are first chairs and second chairs for a reason.

EVVIE. What are you saying?

CATHERINE. When you let yourself dream about what your life's going to be, do you see yourself as a star, Evvie?

EVVIE. I…

CATHERINE. I don't.

EVVIE. …See me as a star?…

CATHERINE. …See either one of us as a star.

EVVIE. Where are you going with this, Catherine?

CATHERINE. Do you see yourself as a soloist? As a first chair?

EVVIE. When I try to see myself, even ten years from now,

I see this big impenetrable cloud. I look at women like Anne-Sophie Mutter, Sarah Chang, Pamela Frank, Midori, Sonnenberg…will I ever be in that league? Do I WANT to be in that league? Is that a life I want, practicing day and night, no life outside music? I don't know, Catherine. I think about finding the time to have love in my life, to have a real partner…somebody who's constant in my life.

CATHERINE. Elliot was constant in your life.

EVVIE. Elliot was a musician. All we did is practice together. And when he wasn't practicing with me, he was practicing alone. I mean somebody *normal*. Somebody who cares about me, worries about me…waits at the dentist while I'm having a filling…I don't know if giving up on a normal life for a life in music is what I want. All I know is that I don't know. That's the truth.

CATHERINE. *(sadly)* Me, too. I don't really know, either. That's me, too. That's what a second chair is: people who don't really know. That's who we are

(and then…)

Where's Elliot, now?

EVVIE. Pittsburgh. Call him. I'm sure he'll be happy to hear from you. I…I…

(While putting resin on her bow. She doesn't finish her thought.)

I'd better get dressed. I have to do this. It got hot in here. I'm sweating. Are you sweating?

CATHERINE. Nerves.

(SFX: We hear – orchestra warming up,)

*(Offstage, as **EVVIE** takes off her bathrobe, hangs it on the rack, stands, momentarily, in her underwear. Suddenly, door swings opens, **MARVIN** pokes in his head.)*

MARVIN. Places, ladies.

*(Looks at **EVVIE**, smiles.)*

Whoopsie!

EVVIE. Come on in, Marv.

(Spins around, slowly, showing **MARVIN** *her body.)*

What do you think?

MARVIN. Nice. Wow! Really really nice. Thank you. I'll walk you to the stage, as soon as you're ready.

EVVIE. I'm ready.

MARVIN. Uh – your dress?

EVVIE. Why? You think I need it?

MARVIN. You're kidding, right?

EVVIE. I am.

(Slips on her dress.)

I'm ready. Cath?

CATHERINE. You go. I'll be right out.

*(***EVVIE** *and* **MARVIN** *exit.* **CATHERINE** *weeps, sits, sobs. Then, she dries her eyes, checks herself in the mirror, exits. orchestra warm-up continues, off.)*

*(***EVVIE** *enters upstage in tight spotlight. We hear – orchestra go silent as* **SERGEI** *taps his baton on music stand. And then* **EVVIE** *begins her 32-bar violin solo, starting* **SERGEI***'s version of Strauss symphony* Ein Heldenleben. *After a few moments of pristine playing, we hear a small mistake. And then, a larger mistake.)*

EVVIE. Shit piss motherfucker!

(Blackout.)

The Play is Over.

THE RACE PLAY

THE RACE PLAY was first presented (January 3-27, 2007) by the Barefoot Theatre Co. at Theatre Row, West 42nd St, NYC, in an evening entitled *ISRAEL HOROVITZ'S NEW SHORTS*, directed by Israel Horovitz, with the following cast:

Evvie	Victoria Malvagno
Todd	Chris Whelan
Bobbi	Kendra Leigh Landon
Jesus	Francisco Solorzano
Annie	Maia Sage Ermansons
Dee Dee	Lynn Cohen
Announcer	Josh Iacovelli
Ernie	Jeremy Brena
Jeannie	Stephanie Janssen

Subsequently, *THE RACE PLAY* premiered in France in March, 2009, presented by the Aleas Theatre, directed by Lea Marie-St.Germain.

THE PEOPLE OF THE PLAY

DEE DEE - 60s-80s.
JEANNIE - 20s-30s.
BOBBI - 20s-30s.
EVVIE - 20s-30s.
ANNIE - 12.
ERNIE - 20s-30s.
TODD - 20s-30s.
JESUS - 20s-30s.

THE TIME OF THE PLAY

The present.

THE PLACE OF THE PLAY

On a road.

"Whenever I feel the need to exercise,
I lie down until the urge passes."
– Oscar Wilde.

(In darkness we hear – male voice [over bullhorn].)

VOICE ON BULLHORN. This is a handicap race, meaning there will be staggered starts based on the runners' best 10-mile time. May we have runners to the starting area, please…

(Music in, pulsating, heroic, something like Vangelis theme for film "Chariots of Fire.")

(Lights fade up on – actors, who instantly transform themselves into runners. They strip out of their street clothes, revealing brightly colored running outfits – shorts and singlets, underneath. There is a race-number pinned to each runner's singlet. If possible, race-numbers should be imprinted "NO KILL 10-MILER.")

(Runners chat as they lace up their running-shoes.)

(Lights now isolate/feature – **DEE DEE SHARP**, *an older woman, chatting with* **JEANNIE RUSH**, *dark-haired, slim, fit.)*

DEE DEE. You don't have an extra couple'a band-aids, do you?

JEANNIE. I do. Blisters?

DEE DEE. Nipples.

JEANNIE. *(handing over two band-aids)* Don't you wear a jog-bra?

DEE DEE. Hell, no! I burned it in 1968!

(As she reaches into singlet, placing band-aids over her nipples…)

Ridiculous, when you're built like me. Just one more thing ta' wash!

JEANNIE. Are you Dee Dee Sharp?

DEE DEE. I am.

JEANNIE. You're a legend.

DEE DEE. Yuh, well, I'd rather be a winner. Who are you?

JEANNIE. Jeannie Rush.

DEE DEE. You just get second in Boston?

JEANNIE. I did, yuh.

DEE DEE. First Boston?

JEANNIE. Uh uh. I got fifth, last year, and eighth, 2 years ago.

DEE DEE. I knew that. I forgot.

(and then...)

I won Boston, twice.

JEANNIE. I know, yuh.

DEE DEE. I won my first Boston with two-thirty-six-twenty and slower, the next year: two-thirty-seven-ten. Times were different in my day. What'd you run? Two-twenty-eight...?

JEANNIE. Two-twenty-three.

DEE DEE. Jesus! What beat you?

JEANNIE. Two-nineteen-fifty.

DEE DEE. Fuckin' ridiculous! What's your best 10-mile time?

JEANNIE. 52 flat.

DEE DEE. I hate you.

VOICE ON BULLHORN. This is a charity event, all proceeds go to create Municipal No-Kill Animal Shelters. We have a distinguished field of international celebrity runners. Please, welcome to the starting line former USA marathon record holder – the incomparable Dee Dee Sharp.

(SFX: Taped applause.)

JEANNIE. Have a good one, Mrs. Sharp.

DEE DEE. Don't ever call me Mrs. Sharp! Too respectful, hurts my feelings.

JEANNIE. Sorry.

DEE DEE. Thanks for the band-aids.

JEANNIE. No probs. Good luck.

DEE DEE. No luck involved. You run the best race you can, same as everybody else. If nobody's lying about their times, the handicaps should bring us all in even-Steven. I'm feelin' pretty good, today, so, I should beat you. Or die tryin'.

(DEE DEE smiles. JEANNIE smiles.)

(SFX: gunshot.)

(DEE DEE starts running [in place]. The race is on.)

(NOTE: Mile markers will appear throughout on-stage race, held up by actors, indicating distance.)

(Music and sounds of breathing should be pre-taped and played throughout the race, as appropriate to the action.)

(During onstage race, from time to time, RUNNERS will change direction by running in place, but turning to face stage-left, as if negotiating a corner, then, change direction, face stage-right, then, change direction, face straight out toward audience. This aspect of the onstage race needs to be choreographed.)

VOICE ON BULLHORN. Welcome Annie Richardson, ladies And gentlemen, 12 years old. USA School Girl Record Holder for 5 miles with a personal best of twenty-eight-twenty.

(SFX: Taped applause. ANNIE RICHARDSON, 12, steps to the line. She seems confused, calls out…)

ANNIE. Is there gonna' be water out on the course?

(SFX: gunshot.)

ANNIE. Oh, shit.

(ANNIE starts running [in place].)

VOICE ON BULLHORN. Open Women to the starting line, please. Welcome three great women's champions… Wisconsin's Jeannie Rush, New York City's own Evvie Piscato and Canadian 10K record-holder Bobbi Lefebvre.

(SFX: Taped applause.)

(JEANNIE is joined on the starting line by EVVIE and BOBBI. EVVIE is small, strong. BOBBI is thin, blonde, fit.)

BOBBI. Nice Boston, Jeannie.

JEANNIE. Thanks, Bob.

BOBBI. How's Ernie?

JEANNIE. He's back runnin'.

BOBBI. I heard.

JEANNIE. He's runnin' today.

BOBBI. I heard.

EVVIE. Either of you got extra band-aids?

JEANNIE. Nipples?

EVVIE. Nipples? You kiddin' me?! Takes more than a band-aid to cover *these* nipples! Start of a blister on my heel.

BOBBI. Ooo. I don't have any. Sorry.

JEANNIE. Damn! I had some extras, but, I gave 'em to Dee Dee Sharp. Sorry.

EVVIE. I'll be okay. My socks are good.

BOBBI. I *heard* Dee Dee Sharp was runnin'. She's a legend.

JEANNIE. She is. Totally. She looks great.

BOBBI. Had her picture on my wall when I was in Junior High…

EVVIE. Why does it say "No Kill" on our race-numbers? Is this charity for, like, death row prisoners?

BOBBI. No, no…It's to stop people from killing animals.

EVVIE. You mean, like, *vegetarians*?

JEANNIE. No kill animal shelters. Dogs and cats.

EVVIE. Dogs and cats? Who the hell eats dogs and cats?

BOBBI. What are you talking about?

  (to **JEANNIE**…*)*

  What is she talking about?

  (SFX: gunshot.)

BOBBI. Shit! That's us!

  (The three women start running [in place]. They are in the race.)

VOICE ON BULLHORN. Open men to the line, please. Welcome Ernie Philbrook, and Todd McCain, top two 10K times in the country…and a special round of applause for Jesus* Lopez, Mexico's National Marathon Champion and Record Holder.

(**ERNIE PHILBROOK**, *30s*, **JESUS LOPEZ** *[*pronounced "hay-soos],"* *20s, and* **TODD MCCAIN**, *30s, jog to the line, stretch out their hamstrings, ready themselves for the race.*)

ERNIE. How's it goin', Todd?

TODD. Excellent. Hamstring okay?

ERNIE. Hundred percent. I think the time off did me good. I'm runnin' my fastest times ever! You?

TODD. I think I can win this.

(**ERNIE** *laughs.*)

ERNIE. How you doin', Jesus?

JESUS. *(thick Mexican accent)* How are your eyes? Can you guys see the front of my shorts?

ERNIE. *(knows what's coming next)* Uh, yuh, Jesus…we can.

TODD. *(knows what's coming next)* Yuh.

JESUS. Then, take a good look, because you'll only be seeing the back of them til this race is over.

(*SFX: gunshot. The* **THREE MEN** *begin running in place.*)

(*Lights shift to –* **EVVIE**, **BOBBI** *and* **JEANNIE**.)

(*MILE MARKER: 3 Miles.*)

EVVIE. We went out too quick!

BOBBI. Feels okay.

EVVIE. I'm struggling.

BOBBI. I'm fine.

JEANNIE. I'm holding back.

BOBBI. Yuh, me, too.

(**EVVIE** *suddenly pulls ahead of* **JEANNIE** *and* **BOBBI**.)

BOBBI. Nice.

JEANNIE. Stay with her.

BOBBI. No probs.

(**JEANNIE** and **BOBBI** pull up even with **EVVIE**.)

(Lights shift to **DEE DEE**, running alone. She speaks directly to audience as she continues to run in place.)

(MILE MARKER: 5 Miles.)

DEE DEE. It's tough getting' old. People keep tellin' you you're lookin' good, but that's bullshit. You're lookin' old, and that sucks like an egg. I used'ta run sub-6 minute miles in a marathon. Now, I'd be lucky to run sub 9s. I s'pose I'm lucky to still be in it at all. Most of the women I knew back then are long gone, either dead from Cancer, or doin' the grandma bit. Myself, I'd rather be dead. I'm gonna run til I drop. When I die, if I could have my way, they'd dig my grave and I'd run to it, dive in, head first, and that'd be that.

(Lights shift to **ERNIE**, **TODD** and **JESUS**, shoulder to shoulder, running full tilt.)

(MILE MARKER: 3 Miles.)

TODD. We're on a 4:20 pace.

ERNIE. A little quick.

JESUS. We're on a 4:20 pace.

TODD. I was sayin'.

JESUS. Slowin' down. We better pick it up.

(With that, **JESUS** speeds up, pulls ahead, slightly. **ERNIE** and **TODD** exchange a worried glance, pick up the pace, catch up/stay with **JESUS**.)

(Lights shift to **ANNIE**, running alone.)

(MILE MARKER: 7 miles.)

ANNIE. I won my age-group in the both the Region and the States, this year. I love runnin'. My parents are pretty good about my doin' it, so long as I keep my grades up. They're getting' divorced. The running helps me when I feel bad, helps me forget the sad stuff. I'd like to make the Olympics when I get older. That's my goal.

(ANNIE *picks up the pace, begins catching up to* DEE DEE. *When* ANNIE *arrives at* DEE DEE, *they share spotlight.*)

ANNIE. Hi.

DEE DEE. I forbid you to pass me.

ANNIE. Excuse me?

DEE DEE. I forbid you to pass me.

ANNIE. I...Okay...I won't pass you...not 'til I need to. Anybody in front of us?

DEE DEE. Nobody.

ANNIE. We're runnin' in *front*?!

DEE DEE. We started about an hour before everybody else.

ANNIE. Still and all.

DEE DEE. They'll be catchin' us, any time now.

ANNIE. You don't think there's any chance we can win it?

DEE DEE. There's always a chance. All the others could get hit by lightning. You never know.

ANNIE. I've got your picture on my wall, Mrs. Sharp.

DEE DEE. *(after a small thoughtful pause)* Is that a tactic?

ANNIE. No, Ma'am.

(*The* THREE WOMAN *start to catch up.*)

ANNIE. Here's the top women, comin' up quick on us.

DEE DEE. *We're* the top women. They're just catchin' up.

EVVIE. This is too quick. I can't hold this pace.

BOBBI. I'm lovin' it.

JEANNIE. I'm strugglin'!

(*And with that,* JEANNIE *pulls ahead, slightly.* EVVIE *and* BOBBI *reel her in. They run shoulder to shoulder, just behind* DEE *and* ANNIE.)

DEE DEE. How old are you?

ANNIE. Twelve.

DEE DEE. What your best 10k time?

ANNIE. 32:47.

DEE DEE. If I had a knife, I would plunge it in your heart.

(Lights shift to – the men.)

(MILE MARKER: 8 Miles.)

TODD. Your wife's right up there.

ERNIE. She's runnin' good, again.

TODD. I was sorry to hear about your baby.

ERNIE. Thanks. We're dealin' with it.

TODD. You got no choice. Margie and I lost our middle daughter, two years ago. You know that?

ERNIE. I did. I'm sorry, man.

TODD. You deal with it. Jesus just lost his mother.

ERNIE. Sorry to hear that, Jesus.

JESUS. Thanks, man. I'm dedicating this race to her.

*(**JESUS** crosses himself, throws kiss to heaven. He then pulls ahead, slightly.)*

*(**ERNIE** and **TODD** pull up even with him.)*

TODD. We're sticking with ya', Jesus.

ERNIE. Why don't we share it, you guys?

TODD. How so?

ERNIE. The three of us…hold hands crossin' the line… share it. It's only a charity race.

JESUS. I like to win, man.

TODD. Who the fuck doesn't like to win, Jesus? It's only a charity race. It's nothing!

JESUS. I still like to win.

TODD. Jesus, get real! I…

(suddenly…)

TODD. *(cont.)* Wow! Check it out! Is that Dee Dee Sharp up front with the kid? Wow! How old is she?

ERNIE. 70-*something*. She's amazing. I'm not runnin' by Dee Dee Sharp. I'll tell you that.

TODD. Me, neither. Great idea, man. Jesus, get with the program. We all hold hands and come in 2nd, cross the line together, right behind Dee Dee Sharp.

ERNIE. She's same age as your mom, I'll bet.

(Beat. **JESUS** *thinks it through.)*

JESUS. Okay. Deal. I'll do it.

(Lights shift to **THE WOMEN.***)*

EVVIE. You guys can have it. I'm dying.

BOBBI. Stay with us, Ev.

JEANNIE. Look at up ahead. Dee Dee Sharp with the kid.

(and then…)

Oh, shit!

BOBBI. What?

JEANNIE. Look behind us.

EVVIE. The boys.

JEANNIE. The boys.

(The **MEN** *catch up shoulder to shoulder with the* **WOMEN.***)*

(MILE MARKER: 9 Miles.)

TODD. Hey, Ev. Lookin' good.

EVVIE. Shut up! I'm dyin'!

ERNIE. *(to* **JEANNIE***)* Hi, honey. How you feelin'?

JEANNIE. Good. Strong.

EVVIE. I'm feelin' horseshit!

JEANNIE. You? How's your hamstring?

ERNIE. Tight, but okay.

BOBBI. Sorry about your mom, Jesus.

JESUS. Thanks.

ERNIE. We're holding hands going in.

BOBBI. Really?

EVVIE. What's this?

ERNIE. We're gonna hold hands and come in tied for Second, behind Dee Dee Sharp.

JEANNIE. I'll do that.

BOBBI. Cool! I'll do that.

EVVIE. I'll do it if you carry me.
TODD. What about the kid?
JEANNIE. I'll talk to her.

> (*And with that,* **JEANNIE** *pulls ahead, pulls up even with* **DEE DEE** *and* **ANNIE**.)

JEANNIE. Hey.

> (**DEE DEE** *doesn't answer, pulls ahead by a few steps.*)

ANNIE. You're Jeannie Rush, right?
JEANNIE. I am.
ANNIE. Great Boston.
JEANNIE. Thanks. You planning to beat her?
ANNIE. Uh uh, no.
JEANNIE. How come?
ANNIE. She forbid me to.
JEANNIE. She did?
ANNIE. She did.
JEANNIE. Good. Don't.
ANNIE. You?
JEANNIE. None of us. We're all goin' in holdin' hands – one step behind her.
ANNIE. Wow! That's great! I promise.
JEANNIE. Good. But, stay with her til the finish…Keep pushin' her.
ANNIE. Got'cha. This is gonna' be cool!

> (**JEANNIE** *slows, deliberately, floats back to other* **RUNNERS**.)

> (*MILE MARKER: 1/2 Mile to go.*)

JEANNIE. It's set. She's with us.
ERNIE. Okay, let's kick it in together. Go.

> (*They pick up the pace, run [in place] faster, faster… They speak in unison…*)

EVVIE. Dyin'…dyin'…dyin'…dyin'…
JEANNIE. Kick…kick…kick…kick…

BOBBI. Quads…burnin'…quads…burnin'…

ERNIE, JESUS, TODD. Kick!…Kick!…Kick!…Kick!…

(Suddenly, Single light on – **DEE DEE**, *steps in front of the Finish Line. She is staggering.)*

DEE DEE. Lungs…burning…no air!…Legs dead…I can't!…I can't!…I can't!…I can't…

*(***DEE DEE** *stops, short of the finish line.* **ANNIE** *screams at her…)*

ANNIE. Kick, Mrs. Sharp! Kick! Don't stop, Mrs. Sharp! Finish! Kick, Mrs. Sharp! Kick! Finish! FINISH!

ALL. Kick, Mrs. Sharp! Kick! Finish! Kick, Mrs. Sharp! Kick! Finish! FINISH!

*(***DEE DEE** *steps over the finish line, finishes the race… wins.)*

DEE DEE. Yes!

(All others now step over line, one step behind her, holding hands, tied for Second place.)

ALL. *YES!!!*

(Blackout.)

The Play is Over.

(12) NEW SHORTS

Photographer: Peter Lindbergh

ABOUT THE AUTHOR

ISRAEL HOROVITZ's 70+ plays have been translated and performed in as many as 30 languages, worldwide.

His best-known plays include *Line* (NYC's longest-running play, now in its 37th year, off-Broadway); *The Indian Wants The Bronx* (which introduced Al Pacino and John Cazale to theatre audiences); *Rats; Morning; The Primary English Class* (which starred Diane Keaton in its New York City premiere); *The Wakefield Plays* (a 7-play cycle composed of *Alfred the Great, Our Father's Failing, Alfred Dies, Hopscotch, The 75th, Stage Directions,* and *Spared*); *The Widow's Blind Date; The Growing Up Jewish Trilogy* (composed of *Today I Am A Fountain Pen, A Rosen By Any Other Name* and *The Chopin Playoffs*); *Park Your Car In Harvard Yard* (a Broadway success starring Jason Robards and Judith Ivey); *North Shore Fish; Fighting Over Beverley; Lebensraum, My Old Lady* (currently playing to SRO houses in Paris and Prague); *Free Gift; Cut-Lady; Stations of the Cross; One Under; 50 Years of Caddieing; Speaking Well of the Dead; Unexpected Tenderness; Fast Hands; Security; A Mother's Love; The Secret of Mme Bonnard's Bath; Sins of the Mother* (premiered February 2009, at Harlequin Theatre, Olympia, WA, and subsequently at Gloucester Stage in August, 2009, and at Florida Stage in January, 2010); *6 Hotels* (composed of *The Audition Play, Fiddleheads and Lovers, Speaking of Tushy, 2nd Violin, Beirut Rocks,* and *The Hotel Play*); and *Compromise*. His newest play, *What Strong Fences Make*, was written in response to Caryl Churchill's *Seven Jewish Children* and is available royalty-free from Samuel French, Inc., and online at www.theatrej.org. *What Strong Fences Make* premiered at the 2009 Boston Theatre Marathon. He is currently completing a new play *The P Word*.

Screenplays include *Author! Author!, The Strawberry Statement* (Prix du Jury, Cannes Film Festival), *Sunshine* (European Academy Award – Best Screenplay), *New York, I Love You*, and EMMY-nominated *James Dean*. Horovitz wrote, directed and performed the award-winning documentary *3 Weeks After Paradise*, shown in the United States on Bravo, now on stage in Paris and Berlin.

Awards include the OBIE (twice); the Prix de Plaisir du Théâtre; The Prix Italia (for radio plays); The Sony Radio Academy Award (for *Man In Snow*); The Writers Guild of Canada Best Screenwriter Award; The Christopher Award; The Drama Desk Award; an Award in Literature of the American Academy of Arts and Letters; The Elliot Norton Prize; a Lifetime Achievement Award from B'Nai Brith; The Literature Prize of Washington College; an honorary Doctorate in Humane Letters from Salem (Massachusetts) State College; Boston Public Library's Literary Lights Award; The Walker Hancock Prize; The Massachusetts Governor's Award; The Arts Award of the City of Gloucester, Massachusetts, honoring Horovitz's 12 Gloucester-based plays.

Horovitz is Founding Artistic Director of Gloucester Stage, and active Artistic Director of the New York Playwrights Lab. He teaches a master class in screenwriting at Columbia University and La Fèmis, France's national film school. Horovitz visits France frequently where he often directs French-language productions of his plays. He is the most-produced American playwright in French theatre history. New York's Barefoot Theatre is celebrating Horovitz's 70th birthday with the creation of The 70/70 Horovitz Project, a year-long event with 70 Horovitz plays having readings and/or productions by theatre companies around the globe. On Horovitz's 70th birthday (March 31, 2009), he was decorated by the French government as Commandeur dans l'Ordre des Arts et des Lettres, France's highest honor awarded to foreign artists.

– *September 2009*

Also by
Israel Horovitz...

A Mother's Love

Barking Sharks

Free Gift

Lebensraum

Man with Bags

Morning (Chiaroscuro)

My Old Lady

Park Your Car in Harvard Yard

Security

Speaking Well of the Dead

Three Weeks After Paradise

Unexpected Tenderness

Please visit our website **samuelfrench.com** for complete descriptions and licensing information

OTHER TITLES AVAILABLE FROM SAMUEL FRENCH

PARK YOUR CAR IN HARVARD YARD
Israel Horovitz

Dramatic Comedy

1f, 1m

Interior

One of the author's acclaimed Gloucester based plays, this resounding success throughout America and Europe starred Judith Ivey and Jason Robards on Broadway. The hilarious and deeply moving tale is about the toughest, meanest teacher to ever set foot in Gloucester High School. Now Jacob Brackish is dying. He advertises for a housekeeper to look after him during his final year and hires mousey, 40 year-old Katherine Hogan, forgetting that he flunked Katherine...and her mother and father...and her recently deceased husband. Kathleen relishes the idea of watching Brackish suffer, but, as his final year passes, memories inspire revelations that redefine the nature of their lives.

"Israel Horovitz has written his best play and roles worthy of Jason Robards, worthy of Judith Ivey, worthy of the blessed Music Box Theatre!"
– *The New Yorker*

"Tickles, provokes, soothes and entertains...The best outing since we drove along with Miss Daisy."
– *New York Magazine*

"A bright and shining gem!"
– *CBS-TV*

SAMUELFRENCH.COM

OTHER TITLES AVAILABLE FROM SAMUEL FRENCH

LEBENSRAUM
Israel Horovitz

Drama

2m, 1f

Unit Set

Using a cast of three to play 40 sharply drawn characters, this bold work of penetrating intelligence is based on the fanciful, explosive idea that a German Chancellor might, as an act of redemption, invite six million Jews to Germany and promise them citizenship and jobs. A resulting scenario unfolds that explores the effects of the policy on Jews and Gentiles with widely varying outlooks: an out of work Jewish dock worker from Massachusetts who brings his Irish wife and his son to Bremerhaven to start a new life, a survivor of Auschwitz who returns to find the woman who betrayed his family to the Nazis, a young German smitten by a Jewish American teenage girl, an unemployed German laborer and scores of others. The actors make quicksilver changes from one character to the next, occasionally using masks or character cut outs to enhance the transformations. The logical progression of this artfully drawn script raises the terrifying possibility that history may repeat.

"Powerful and touching."
– *The New York Times*

SAMUELFRENCH.COM